# A MOST
# ACCURSED
# RELIGION

Published by Spring Publications, Inc.
28 Front Street, Putnam, CT 06260
www.springpublications.com

Distributed by The Continuum International Publishing Group
www.continuumbooks.com

First Edition 2005

Printed in Canada

Cover design by white.room productions, New York

Library of Congress Cataloging-in-Publication Data

Mogenson, Greg, 1959–
  A most accursed religion : when a trauma becomes God / Greg Mogenson.— 1st ed.
    p. cm.
  Summary: "Despite its title, this book is not about theology. When a psychologist
writes of God, he must do so within the confines of his own field of inquiry, the psyche.
Mogenson's aim is to focus attention on the religious dimension of the psychology of
those overwhelming events we describe as traumatic"—Provided by publisher.
  ISBN-13: 978-0-88214-552-5 (pbk. original : alk. paper)
  ISBN-10: 0-88214-552-5 (pbk. original : alk. paper)
  1. Psychology, Religious. 2. Traumatism. 3. God—Wrath. 4. Life change events—
Religious aspects. 5. Accidents—Religious aspects. 6. Disasters—Religious aspects.
I. Title.

BL53.M64 2005
200.1'9—dc22
                                       2005032999

∞The paper used in this publication meets the minimum requirements of the
American National Standard for Information Sciences—Permanence of Paper
for Printed Library Materials, ANSI Z39.48-1992.

# A MOST
# ACCURSED
# RELIGION
WHEN A TRAUMA BECOMES GOD

## GREG MOGENSON

SPRING PUBLICATIONS, INC.
PUTNAM, CONNECTICUT

I wish to express my gratitude to all those who have supported me in the work that is represented in these pages:

Ross Woodman, Michael Mendis, Rita Mendis-Mogenson,
James Hillman, Mary Helen Sullivan, David L. Miller,
Peter VanKatwyk, Susan Estabrooks, and Angela Sheppard.

— G.M.

The author and publisher gratefully acknowledge permission to reprint as follows:

Section III of "Esthétique du Mal," from *The Palm at the End of the Mind: Selected Poems and a Play* by Wallace Stevens, Vintage Books, originally published by Alfred A. Knopf, Inc. © by Holly Stevens.

The sections "The Infectious Savior," "Romanticism," and "Into Her Own Hands" of this book, previously published in "Stepping Out of the Great Code," by Greg Mogenson, in *Voices: The Art and Science of Psychotherapy*, vol. 21, no. 3/4, Fall 1985/Winter 1986. © *Voices*. Reprinted with permission. The section, "Escaping to the Angels," previously published as "Escaping to the angels: a note on the passing of the manic defence," by Greg Mogenson, in *The Journal of Analytical Psychology*, January 1996, 41, 1, pp. 77–80.

# INTRODUCTION

THIS BOOK, despite its title, is not a theology book. It is not a book about God *as* God. In identifying the words "God" and "trauma" in the subtitle, my aim is to focus attention on the *religious dimension* of the *psychology* of those overwhelming events we describe as traumatic. When a psychologist writes of God he must do so within the confines of his own field of inquiry, the psyche. Like Jung who, in his own way, tackled themes related to the one facing us here, our references to "God" in these pages will be to the *imago dei*, the God-image or God-complex — not to God in an ontological sense. [1]

Images and fantasies of God abound in psychic life and have a determining effect upon its movement, regardless of whether a God 're-ally exists' or not. From the standpoint of theology, a standpoint that attempts to start with God even as psychology starts with psyche, the contention that "God" is a synonym for trauma will seem grossly reductionistic. After all, to the theologian and the believer, God may be thought of as being in all things even as He is the creator of all things. Again, let me stress: this book is not a theology book. My aim is not to reduce the God(s) of religion and theology to a secularized category of psychopathology, but rather, to raise the secularized term "trauma" to the immensity of the religious categories which, in the form of images, are among its guiding fictions.

Whether a divine being really exists or not, the psychological fact remains that we tend to experience traumatic events *as if* they were in some sense divine. Just as God has been described as transcendent and unknowable, a trauma is an event which transcends our capacity to experience or reckon with it. [2] Compared to the finite nature of the traumatized soul, the traumatic event seems infinite, all-powerful, and wholly other. Again, we cannot say that traumatic events literally possess these properties, but only that the traumatized soul propitiates them as if they did.

Human affliction has always been a problem for theology. Indeed, the question — "How do we reconcile suffering and pain with a loving God?" — has proven to be among the richest questions sustaining theological reflection. Theology's approach to the problem, of course, has mainly been in the genre of theodicy. Faithful to a benevolent conception of God, theology has attempted to justify the ways of God to age upon age of men and women who have been shattered by events which have lent the created world a malevolent cast. Barth, Tillich, C.S. Lewis, Hans Küng: theologian after theologian has attempted to minister to the interminable struggle of the soul with pain.

Despite the comparisons drawn between the analyst's couch and the priest's confessional, the difference between the two is perhaps more significant. When he examines the engagement of theology, the psychologist cannot help wondering if theology has placed the needs of the soul secondary to its own need to justify the ways of its root metaphor "God." Even those theologians who fastidiously attempt to keep themselves open to the phenomenon of suffering work from an essentially closed perspective in that their thinking is committed from the outset to the service of what they already believe on instinct. For the theologian, the premier psychological question — "What does the soul want?" — takes a backseat to the premier theological question — "What does God demand?"

This "God first, psyche second" priority is not merely academic; it occurs, as well, in the biblical account of man's relationship with God. When we read the Bible, particularly the Old Testament, we meet a God who demands the submissive obedience of the soul to His awesome knowledge and power and who is prepared to test this obedience through torture. Like a cat playing with a mouse, the Creator plays with His creature Job.[3] When Job enquires about God's motives in torturing him, the divine terrorist answers him out of a storm:

> Will you really annul My judgement?
> Will you condemn Me
> That you may be justified?
> Or do you have an arm like God,
> And can you thunder with a voice like His?
> Adorn yourself with eminence and dignity;
> And clothe yourself with honor and majesty.
> Pour out the overflowings of your anger
> And look on everyone who is proud, and make him low.
>
> (Job 40:8–11)

The controlling metaphor of theology is an overpowering metaphor, a metaphor that literalizes itself in terms of the God-given goodness of affliction and evil. Like Job terrified before the mightiness of God, the theologian, working from a metaphor which denies its relativity as a metaphor, must suppress the objections of his suffering soul. "Behold, I am insignificant; what can I reply to Thee?" (Job 40:4).

The psychological move from theology's soul-transcending God to the God-complex that stirs within the soul revolutionizes our conception of the traumatized soul. Psychological reflection reverses the "God first, psyche second" priority. While the theologian writing his theodicy does so with his mouth covered, ever on guard, like Job, lest his representation of suffering seem impious to his Maker, the psychologist tries to amplify the voice of the afflicted psyche. Like Jung in his *Answer to Job*, he must write without inhibition if he is "to give expression to the shattering emotion which the unvarnished spectacle of divine savagery and ruthlessness produces in us."[4]

The theologian, of course, is as skeptical about the humanism of psychology as the psychologist is of the traumatized and traumatizing theism of the theologian. If Man were truly the measure of all things then presumably he would be able to be the measure of his sufferings as well. But the world is bigger than Man. We exist in a creation that transcends us in every direction. If today Man's knowledge and power rival the knowledge and power which Yahweh lorded over Job, will we prove any more judicious than He in our administration of it? The countdown to the Apocalypse has now started, and it is Man the humanist whose finger is on the button, not God.

The psychologist, especially the imaginal psychologist, is not so sure. He agrees with the theologian in his criticism of humanism, but wonders if it is not, after all, a God-image that has its finger on the button. For the psychologist, Man is not the measure of soul for precisely the same reason as God is not its measure. For him, both are metaphors that contain within themselves their own characteristic styles of literalizing. In order to stay psychological, psychology must take the metaphor "human" no more literally and, yet, no less seriously than it takes the metaphor "God." As James Hillman has put it:

... of these notions, psyche and human, psyche is the more embracing, for there is nothing of man that soul does not contain,
affect, influence, or define. Soul enters into all of man and is
in everything human. Human existence is psychological before
it is anything else — economic, social, religious, physical. In
terms of logical priority, all realities (physical, social, religious)
are inferred from psychic images or fantasy presentations to a
psyche. In terms of empirical priority, before we are born into
a physical body or a social world, the fantasy of the child-to-
come is a psychic reality, influencing the "nature" of the subsequent events.

But the statement that soul enters into everything human
cannot be reversed. Human does not enter into all of soul, nor
is everything psychological human. Man exists in the midst
of psyche; it is not the other way around. Therefore, soul is
not confined by man, and there is much of psyche that extends
beyond the nature of man. The soul has inhuman reaches. [5]

Just as psychology must distinguish its engagement from theology in
order to remain psychological, it must distinguish itself from humanism
as well. Although humanism and theism have recently taken to founding their identity on their prudence in not committing the errors they
attribute to each other, refusing the genre of theodicy does not necessarily mean that one has chosen the genre of humanism in its stead. Despite the powerful influence of Christianity, and Tertullian's declaration
that the soul is naturally Christian, psychology need not crucify itself between the opposites of God and Man. The soul's sufferings cannot be
divided into the despair of Christ forsaken to his humanity without re-
mainder any more than its joys can be divided evenly into his reunion
with God. The logos of the psyche, as Heraclitus wrote six centuries before
Christ, resides in its own depths. When we take up the term "psyche" or
"soul" as our root metaphor a *process* of reflection begins, which constantly
deepens itself by deliteralizing itself. Psychological reflection above all
knows itself, even if the reflective moment of that knowing changes it, re-
quiring yet other reflective acts *ad infinitum*. Psychologically speaking, what
we see and declare one moment may be re-valued and re-visioned the
next, as the subjective standpoint backing our perception becomes as well
the object of reflection.

Here we do well to remember Hillman's usage of the term "soul":

> By soul I mean . . . a perspective rather than a substance, a
> viewpoint toward things rather than a thing itself. This per-
> spective is reflective; it mediates events and makes differences
> between ourselves and everything that happens. Between us
> and events, between the doer and the deed, there is a reflec-
> tive moment — and soul-making means differentiating this
> middle ground.[6]

The terms "human" and "divine" become more soulful when we see
them also as perspectives. Taken "as if," they, too, can mediate events
and make differences. Taken literally, however, they pre-empt the soul's
capacity to distinguish itself from events sufficiently to experience them.
On the one hand, we lose soul to the human-all-too-human and, on the
other, to a God before whom one may have no other "as if" structures.
Identification either way produces unconsciousness — totalized vision,
white-out. When a perspective is allowed to monopolize awareness it
creates the world in its own image while remaining blind to its own
stance. Like an Elohim, a Jehovah, or a Yahweh, it is utterly unable to
see itself. Psychological awareness requires a context, "a perception of
differences,"[7] a variety of perspectives. If we cannot say what a thing is
"like," we are held in its thrall and cannot incorporate it as an experience.
Jung, who was as much a therapist of Christianity as he was a therapist
of the psyche, makes this point with regard to what he saw as theology's
unreflective use of the term "God":

> . . . statements made about [transcendent reality] are so bound-
> lessly varied that with the best of intentions we cannot know
> who is right. The denominational religions recognized this
> long ago and in consequence each of them claims that it is the
> only true one and, on top of this, that it is not merely a human
> truth but the truth directly inspired and revealed by God. Every
> theologian speaks simply of "God," by which he intends it to
> be understood that his "god" is *the* God. But one speaks of the
> paradoxical God of the Old Testament, another of the incar-
> nate God of Love, a third of the God who has a heavenly bride,
> and so on, and each criticizes the other but never himself.[8]

A principle theme we shall pursue through the pages of this book is the impact on the soul of monotheistic theology's no-name God. What happens to the soul when it reflects upon its problems in the terms of so absolute and generic a spirit? Does it assist the soul in its soul-making? Does it help the soul to "mediate events" and to make "differences between ourselves and everything that happens"? Or does it galvanize those events with the numinous sheen of the unapproachably holy? Does invoking the name of the Lord preserve the overwhelming quality of overwhelming events, embedding the traumatic?

If "image *is* psyche," [9] as Jung says in one of his definitions, then a God without images is a God without soul. Though the biblical God prohibits the making of graven images, adherence to this injunction is no guarantee against the production of false gods. On the contrary, almost anything can reign as a deity if it is left as image-less and self-identical as He. *Whatever we cannot imagine, we reify and deify.* Whatever we cannot inhabit psychologically, we propitiate with religious responses. It is not just that God is unknowable and unimaginable; it is that we reach for "God" most earnestly when imagination fails us, that is, when we, like Him, are without soul. To stand before an event for which we have no metaphors is to stand in the tabernacle of the Lord. Like Moses before the bush that burned and yet was not consumed, the soul falls down prostrate before whatever it is unable to relativize into images. The reverence displayed, however, amounts to the soul's undoing. Dissociated from its own self-movement by the action of an external cause, soul is soul no longer.

Failures of the imagination are not uncommon. After the miscarriage, the break-up, or the tragic car accident, we may find ourselves utterly unable to imagine our lives forward. The soul, spellbound by events which have overwhelmed it, cannot lay hold of its other images. Night after night the same dreams, the exact same scenes, return. Wounded by an event, the disabled soul is unable to make distinctions *within* the event. Consciousness atrophies. Vietnam continues as before, regardless of the fact that the boys are home. Is it not at this time, in our times of intolerable affliction, that we are most likely to reflect in terms of God? Is not a trauma of some sort, physical or otherwise, the principle background of religious conversion? When we examine closely the specifics of the events which have overwhelmed us, we find them to be the causes — efficient, material, formal, and final — of our so-called first cause, God. Yes, the image-less God is an image *for us*, albeit an intolerable image. The jungle fire-fight, the early morning rape, the speeding automobile of the drunk driver — all these images may be God images if, like God, they create us in their image, after their likeness.

So long as the overwhelming event is at least slightly larger than the soul's capacity to absorb it, it will be construed as infinite. It is not just that one theologian "speaks of the paradoxical God of the Old Testament, another of the incarnate God of Love, a third of the God who has a heavenly bride"; the God-image which possesses the soul can also be a severed spinal cord, an autonomous sex drive, the domineering will of an abusive parent. The AIDS epidemic is another example. In the last few decades a new denomination of converts has trembled in its thrall. Like the image-less God, the HIV virus changes its genetic make-up faster than its medical priesthood can develop a vaccine. The Bible re-constellates. Sodom and Gomorrah falls once more. Deuteronomy re-writes itself in the lineage of our hematological love histories. New moralities are passed down. An Apocalypse is prophesied. [10]

The traumatized soul, the soul that has stopped "mediating events" and "mak[ing] differences between [itself] and everything else," is a soul in need of therapy. Psychotherapy, at least as I shall be presenting the practice, consists of precisely what the roots of the word imply. First and foremost, psychotherapy is a *caring* for the *soul*. The Greek root "*therapeutae*" suggests "an attendant, servant, physician." [11] A therapist of the psyche is one who attends, serves, and doctors the images of the psyche, the images of the soul.

Again, the contrast between the analyst's couch and the priest's confessional stands out markedly. Unlike the priest, the psychotherapist is not in the business of *saving* souls. Indeed, from his perspective, conversion is a main symptom of traumatic disturbance. The soul, unable to mediate or differentiate events, conforms to the ordinances of an event as if it were the spirit.

Nowhere is this background to conversion more evident than in the ministries of the television evangelists. Every morning of the week, evangelical preachers invite the drug addict and the prostitute, the single mother and the sex addict to give their souls to Jesus. Pain, misery, and the wages of sin dominate these programs as if religion were unthinkable except as a balm to suffering. By the end of the show — and these programs can be showy — telephones ring off their hooks and large numbers from the studio audience, running "more like a man flying from something that he dreads than one who sought the thing he loved," [12] hasten down to the altar in response to the preacher's call.

Watching these antics the theologian and the sophisticated theist will quickly agree with the psychologist's critical viewpoint and hasten to mark themselves different. But still the phenomenon remains: the traumatized soul, seeking solace through conversion, gives itself over to the spirit *and ceases to be psychological.* Out of the frying pan of the event that it could not assimilate, the soul enters into the fire of a transcending spirituality that it is even less able to absorb. Like the stillness after the storm, or the tranquillity following the electro-convulsive therapy, a state of grace ensues. The totalized metaphor of God suffering with and for man through His crucified Son brings salvation to the soul. Like Paul, the traumatized soul now rejoices in its sufferings and does its share "on behalf of His Body (which is the church) in filling up that which is lacking in Christ's afflictions" (Col. 1:24). But — and here is the rub, at least as the psychologist sees it — *any metaphor that offers itself as the ultimate metaphor is no metaphor at all.* The soul's mediating function, knocked around by events it can not relativize into images, is completely knocked out when "saved" by the metaphor that ends all metaphors: Christ as vicarious atonement.

In pointing out the grass-roots popularity of conversion, I do not intend to imply that the soul is naturally Christian. Nor do I wish to imply, following Jung, that religions are "psychotherapeutic systems." [13] My point is simply that trauma is inherently religious. The soul's functioning can be as held in thrall by the monolithic perspectives of the spirit that would save it as by the monolithic brutalities of matter that afflict it.

Where the priest would minister to the salvation of soul, the psychotherapist would seek to restore the soul to its own activity. Therapy of
the psyche involves a doctoring of the soul's capacity to make differences
between itself and matter, on the one hand, and between itself and spirit
on the other. For soul, as the Platonic psychologists have described it, is
the realm between matter and spirit. Rarer than the world of matter and
more embodied than the world of spirit, it is a world of images which reflect, mirror, and mediate the ways in which matter and spirit are related.
What is the matter with spirit and what is the spirit of matter? — these
are the questions to which the soul makes its metaphorical replies.

When the perspective of the soul is lost, we are given over to the
compulsions of matter and the fanaticisms of the spirit. Fundamental-
ism and ideology, as if conditioned by the most primitive stimulus/re-
sponse causality, replace the valuing, imagining process through which
events become experiences. Like the molested child who later becomes
a child molester, the traumatized soul devoutly repeats the events which
have proven so transfixing for it, as if trying to recover its capacity to
experience and feel.

The psychotherapist's goal is not to spirit suffering away through
some secular intervention or to turn suffering into spirit — as the priest
would prefer as he shepherds the afflicted soul along the Way of the
Cross. The psychotherapist is on the side of *experience*. His task is to restore to the soul its capacity for experiencing events. As Hillman has
written, "*Whenever treatment directly neglects the experience as such and hastens to
reduce or overcome it, something is being done against the soul. For experience is the soul's
one and only nourishment.*" [14]

Psychotherapy heals the soul by insisting that it experience its afflictions within the discrete proportions of the images in which those afflictions reflectively reside. Neurotic suffering, as Jung said, is inauthentic
suffering, [15] a suffering estranged from the images of the soul's actual life.
It is in connection with this issue that religious conversion and the theology of vicarious atonement become matters of clinical concern. After
two thousand years of Christian salvation, the story of Christ crucified
is too often substituted for the authenticity of one's own images, despite
the fact that not every wound is a crucifixion. [16] It does not even matter

whether we are Christian or not. The dramaturgy of the Passion can still upstage the soul's relationship to its own images and cause it to suffer against the wrong background. Ironically, a large part of the job of psychotherapy (and a main concern of this book) is releasing the soul from the collective neurosis which in the guise of religion sanctifies estrangement of the soul from its own images and experiences.

To conclude these introductory remarks, a few words about the format of the book are in order. Although organized into chapters, the book consists essentially of a long series of short essays, each more or less independent of the others. When one considers that a main feature of traumatic disturbances is the tendency to repeat the traumatic event again and again in diverse situations, my reason for writing a series of variations on a theme will become apparent. By writing in a style that parallels the traumatized soul's compulsion to repeat what it is unable to remember, I aim to accentuate a therapeutic possibility within the repetition compulsion itself. When a trauma has varied its theme in a sufficient number of situations, a context may coagulate around it in whose terms the event at its core can be relativized, particularized, and experienced. But in order for a trauma to break free from the spell in which it is transfixed, the imaginative process, which it has unconsciously literalized into compulsive behavior, must be mirrored back to it in imaginative ways.

Here, though with a contemporary twist, we are following the classical Freudian account of the utilization of compulsive repetitions in analysis. In Freud's view, a tactic of analytic technique is to interpret the patient's behavior inside and outside the therapy hour as "his way of remembering"[17] repressed material. What the patient refuses to remember in the analysis or to retrieve through free association he will tend to behave. "The greater the resistance," writes Freud, "the more extensively will expressing in action (repetition) be substituted for recollecting."[18] By "curbing the patient's compulsion to repeat . . . and turning it into a motive for remembering,"[19] the analyst "struggles with the patient to keep all the impulses, which he would like to carry into action within the boundaries of the mind . . ."[20]

The contemporary twist we shall be giving to this account is that where Freud spoke of "remembering" or "recollecting" we shall speak of *imagining.* The psychoanalytic motto "we act out what we can't remember" becomes for us "we are determined by the literalness of events (physical, emotional, intellectual, social, etc.), which we cannot imagine." Memory, or *memoria* as it was once called, is a form of imagination.[21] What it recalls into the present is always, in part, a function of the perspective currently dominating the present. Though we tend to reify history, thinking of it as what "really happened" in the past, history is not static. Inasmuch as it touches us experientially, it must enter into the imaginative modes of recollection, thereby becoming psycho-history, a history of soul. The very substance of what we remember or fail to remember changes as we, its historians, change. Even traumatic events, events which once possessed the mind and galvanized the memory, can be re-written by "keep[ing] all the impulses which [we] would like to carry into action within the boundaries" of imaginative reflection.

There is another reason for writing in the variations-on-a-theme format. In order for psychological writing to stay psychological, it must eschew the monolithic tendencies of the positivistic spirit of scientism and theology. Psychological life, like a dream series or a conversation that meanders amongst the soul's complexes, is radically discontinuous — even with itself. One theory can never encompass the soul's bounty. Soul-making is an endless process, and the events that we make into soul one day may have to be re-made the next. Writing a series of vignettes reflects that psychological writing must be as endless as the depths of the soul itself. Indeed, were we to become monolithic, were we to stop the soul's ongoing imagining activity with a final truth, we would simply be replacing the traumatic content with an equally unabsorbable didactic content. In the name of soul-making, we would then actually be contributing to vicarious religion. We would be writing doctrinal theology. Events would not be turned into experiences that lend the soul substance while at the same time allowing it to imagine on. They would be turned into dogmas, fixed meanings, and psychoanalytic cult reactions.

But selling out the soul to the viewpoint of something more literal is not the answer to the problem of alleviating the soul's distress. There is a relief that comes not from simple answers and the courage of conviction but from increased ambivalence, complexity and, as Nietzsche taught, the courage to criticize one's own convictions. This is the soul's way. It heals by differentiating problems, by mediating and making differences within them. As Poul Anderson has said, "I have yet to see any problem, however complicated, which when looked at in the right way did not become still more complicated."[22] The psyche's way is not a way of simplicity, but of complexity; not a way of certainty, but of imagination. In the writing that follows we shall be attempting to follow this way with soul.

1. This holds true even when our references are to God-images drawn from biblical sources. While the believer may read the Bible to gain knowledge of the ontological God, the psychologist reads the Bible to gain knowledge of the soul. For him the Bible is a psychological document.

2. This sentence is not a logical deduction. I am *not* saying that since God is transcending and since trauma is transcending, *therefore* God is a trauma. With the same reasoning one could argue that since Africans and umbrellas are both black, Africans are umbrellas. My sentence is intended as a *description* of a *psychological identification,* which exists between overwhelming events and the categories theology would reserve for deity. The psyche is irrational. It constantly makes inferences and deductions that philosophy and theology would judge to be mistaken. But these connections and identifications are the *facts* of the psyche, regardless of their value to other disciplines. The psychologist's concern is with the brute fact that the traumatized soul is a theologizing soul — not with the merits of that resultant "theology" as theology.

3. This reading of Job presupposes Jung's reading in his *Answer to Job.* The cat and mouse metaphor is his as well. This essay is included in volume 11 of C.G. Jung, *The Collected Works,* trans. R.F.C. Hull, eds. H. Read, M. Fordham, G. Adler, W. McGuire, Bollingen Series XX, vols. 1–20 (Princeton: Princeton University Press and London: Routledge and Kegan Paul, 1953 ff.). All further references to Jung's *Collected Works* (CW) will be by volume and paragraph numbers.

4. C.G. Jung, CW 11: 561.

5. James Hillman, *Re-Visioning Psychology* (New York: Harper & Row, 1975), p. 173.

6. Ibid. p. x.

7. C.G. Jung, CW 14: 603.

8. C.G. Jung, CW 14: 781.

9. C.G. Jung, CW 13: 75.

10. Perhaps, since I first wrote this paragraph in the 1980's, the AIDS epidemic has moved into that phase of religion that the Canadian author Pierre Berton, writing with reference to the United Church of Canada, has called "the comfortable pew."

11. Gary V. Hartman, "Psychotherapy: An Attempt at Definition," *Spring 1980*: 91.

12. William Wordsworth, "Lines Composed a Few Miles above Tintern Abbey," in *The Penguin Book of English Romantic Verse,* ed. David Wright (Harmondsworth: Penguin Books, 1968), p. 111.

13. C.G. Jung, CW 16: 390.

14, James Hillman, *Suicide and the Soul* (Dallas: Spring Publication, 1976), p. 23.

15. C.G. Jung, CW II: 129.

16. Cf. James Hillman, Re-Visioning Psychology, pp. 95–99.

17. Sigmund Freud, "Further Recommendations in the Technique of Psycho-Analysis: Recollection, Repetition and Working Through," Collected Papers, ed. Ernest Jones, trans. Joan Riviere, 5 vols. (London, The Hogarth Press, 1950), 2: 370. All further references to Freud's Collected Papers (CP) will be cited by volume and page numbers.

18. Ibid.

19. Ibid., p. 374.

20. Ibid., p. 373.

21. Cf. James Hillman, Re-Visioning Psychology, p. 18.

22. Cited by K.D. Newman in "Counter-Transference and Consciousness," Spring 1980: 117.

chapter one

# THE TRAUMA-GOD

Howl ye; for the day of the LORD is at hand: it shall come as a destruction from the Almighty, Therefore shall all hands be faint, and every man's heart shall melt. And they shall be afraid: pangs and sorrows shall take hold of them; they shall be in pain as a woman travaileth: they shall be amazed one at another; their faces shall be as flames. Behold, the day of the LORD cometh, cruel both with wrath and fierce anger, to lay the land desolate; and he shall destroy the sinners thereof out of it. For the stars of heaven and the constellations thereof shall not give their light: the sun shall be darkened in his going forth, and the moon shall not cause her light to shine. And I will punish the world for their evil, and the wicked for their iniquity; and I will cause the arrogance of the proud to cease, and will lay low the haughtiness of the terrible. I will make a man more precious than fine gold; even a man than the golden wedge of Ophir. Therefore I will shake the heavens, and the earth shall remove out of her place, in the wrath of the LORD of hosts, and in the day of his fierce anger. And it shall be as the chased roe, and as a sheep that no man taketh up: they shall every man turn to his own people, and flee every one into his own land. Every one that is found shall be thrust through; and every one that is joined unto them shall fall by the sword. Their children also shall be dashed to pieces before their eyes; their houses shall be spoiled, and their wives ravished. Behold, I will stir up the Medes against them, which shall not regard silver; and as for gold, they shall not delight in it. Their bows also shall dash the young men to pieces; and they shall have no pity of the fruit of the womb; their eye shall not spare children.

(Isaiah 13:6–18)

## The Wrath of God

WHEN WE READ THE BIBLE, we are as impressed with the dark side of God as with His light side. In Isaiah 45:7, the Lord describes himself as "One forming light and creating darkness, causing well-being and creating calamity." In the second of the Ten Commandments, God declares himself a "jealous God" and threatens to visit "the iniquity of the fathers on the children of the third and the forth generations" of those who break His law (Ex. 20:5). Again and again, as repetitiously as the throbbing of an intense pain, we are told that the Lord is "vengeful" and turns His "wrath" upon those who resist His will. When Moses failed to circumcise his son, God became enraged and attempted to kill him (Ex. 4:24). When Jonah shirked the call to cry against the sins of the city of Nineveh, God had him swallowed into the belly of a whale until he was terrified into submission (Jonah 1:17).

Even with those who had been faithful to Him, the biblical record portrays God's behavior as sadistic. Though God characterizes his servant Job as a man who more than any other has been "blameless and upright . . . fearing God and turning away from evil" (Job 1:8), He takes up Satan's challenge: "Does Job fear God for nothing?" (Job 1:9). In order to be sure that Job's faithfulness is not simply fair-weather loyalty, God agrees with Satan's proposal to test him with tribulations. A tornado is dispatched, which kills Job's sons and daughters (Job 1:19), and he is covered with boils and sores (Job 2:7). Though the innocent victim of these heaven-sent afflictions, Job laments but does not cry out against his Maker (Job 16:12–17):

> I was at ease, and He broke me asunder;
> He seized me by the neck and dashed me to pieces;
> He set me up as His target, His archers surround me.
> He slashes open my kidneys, and does not spare;
> He pours out my gall on the ground.
> He breaks me with breach upon breach;

He runs upon me like a warrior.
I have sewed sackcloth upon my skin,
and have laid my strength in the dust.
My face is red with weeping, and on my eyelids is deep
darkness; although there is no violence in my hands,
and my prayer is pure.

When God, in the form of a whirlwind and storm, finally speaks to the traumatized Job, He righteously declares to him that it would be ridiculous and blasphemous to question or protest his sufferings. "Where were you," asks God, "when I laid the foundation of the earth!" (Job 38:4). In two long speeches God reminds Job of His omnipotent power and reproaches him for having the audacity to even faintly question his treatment. He shows Job the monsters Behemoth (Job 40:15) and Leviathan (Job 41:1) and asks him how he could dare to question his Creator when he cannot even contend with his fellow creatures.

Throughout the Old Testament, references to the might and fury of the Lord abound. In Jeremiah 45:4–5 the Lord says:

Behold, what I have built I am breaking down, and what I have planted I am plucking up, that is, the whole land. And do you seek great things for yourself? seek them not; For, behold, I am bringing evil upon all flesh . . .

In Psalm 44 the psalmist laments to God:

All this has come upon us, but we have not forgotten Thee, and we have not dealt falsely with Thy covenant, our heart has not turned back, and our steps have not deviated from Thy way, yet Thou has crushed us in a place of jackals, and covered us with the shadow of death. If we had forgotten the name of our God, or extended our hands to a strange god; . . . But for Thy sake we are killed all day long; we are considered as sheep to be slaughtered. Arouse Thyself, why dost Thou sleep, Lord? . . . Why dost Thou hide Thy face, and forget our affliction and our oppression? For our soul has sunk down into the dust; our body cleaves to the earth. Rise up, be our help, and redeem us for the sake of Thy lovingkindness.

The God of the Hebrew-Christian tradition is the single source both of affliction and lovingkindness. When the children of Israel suffer tribulation, it is because God has willed that it be so, and when they wish redemption from their sufferings, it is to that same one God they must turn. To love the Lord to His satisfaction requires that we bow down before Him in fear, for, as the Book of Job teaches, God demands our complete allegiance and is prepared to go to the most inhuman lengths to test it. Nowhere, it seems, are we more immediately in the presence of the Lord than when we are wracked with pain or covered with boils. God is both the world-destroying deluge and the rainbow which follows after it. In His wrath He destroys us, and in His mercy He spares us from His wrath. He is the author of both Good and Evil, pain and pleasure, and of life and death. He works by earthquake and volcano, whirlwind and storm, pestilence, famine and the atrocities of war. His is the name we ascribe to whatever overwhelms us (lest we be accused of having other gods before Him). His ordinances are the ordinances of trauma. His authority is the authority of trauma. All vengeance belongs to Him, and He is in all things that seem to punish, afflict, or spare us.

The religious moment, the moment of the deity, is the moment of tribulation or deliverance from tribulation. When the Hebrews invoked God, they were aware of this dread paradox and appealed to His benevolent side. In Psalm 9 we are told that "The Lord also will be a refuge for the oppressed, a refuge in times of trouble." In Psalm 107, similarly, God is associated with the termination of affliction:

> Then they cried unto the Lord in their trouble, and He saved them out of their distresses. He brought them out of darkness and the shadow of death, and brake their bands in sunder. Oh that men would praise the Lord for His goodness, and for His wonderful works to the children of men! . . . Who so is wise, and will observe these things, even they shall understand the lovingkindness of the Lord. (13–15, 43)

When we read passages about the lovingkindness of the Lord, we get the distinct impression that the Psalmist "protesteth too loudly." These passages, though often clearly inspired by the joy of deliverance, just as often seem to be the propitiating reaction formations of men "that hath seen affliction by the rod of His wrath" (Lamentations 3:1). The story of Job gives especially clear witness to this tactic of the suffering creature to love into kindness the power which vanquishes it:

> O that Thou wouldest hide me in the grave, that thou wouldest keep me secret, until Thy wrath be past, that Thou wouldest appoint me a set time and remember me! If a man die, shall he live again? all the days of my appointed time I will wait, till my change come.
> (Job 14:13–14)

Jeremiah invokes and propitiates God in a similar fashion:

> The Lord is my portion, saith my soul: therefore will I hope in Him. The Lord is good unto them that wait for Him, to the soul that seeketh Him. It is good that a man should both hope and quietly wait for salvation of the Lord . . . For the Lord will not cast off for ever: But though He cause grief, yet will he have compassion according to the multitude of His mercies. For He doth not afflict willingly nor grieve the children of men.
> (Lamentations 3:24–26, 31–33)

The wrath of God and the kindness of God are complexly interwoven. When we are crushed and broken by an overwhelming event, we experience firsthand what the ancient Hebrews knew as the rod of His wrath. A natural piety is called into play, a piety of terror and dread. Brought low, broken asunder, we prostrate ourselves before the stimulus that threatens to annihilate us as if before our Maker. Typically, there is a moral moment. It seems that we are being punished. But what are we being punished for? What have we done to warrant this affliction? We search ourselves for sin. If we can find ourselves guilty of some error or indiscretion, our suffering will at least make sense and we can set about making our atonement.

Often, however, we can find no sin and our affliction seems quite senseless. But here, too, we are easily given over to piety. As the pain increases so, too, does our sense of relationship to an omnipotent being. As the persistence of our suffering mocks our ability to understand it within the categories of our usual existence, our sense of relationship to a wholly other will and purpose grows. Gradually, conversion dawns. The ontology of the event that traumatizes us upstages our own ontology. In order to survive, we enter into the route of that which afflicts us and allow ourselves to be re-created by it. Submitting ourselves to its epistemology, we become the keepers of its law. "Glory, Glory, Glory, for the Lord, God, Omnipotent reigneth!" As piously as the phobic patient propitiates the eliciting stimulus of his phobia, we propitiate the overwhelming event that has transcended us, acknowledging its holiness. Only in the eye of the storm do we feel safe. Only in those ritualized observances that the faithless call our "symptoms" are we the children of God.

## The Suffering God

Whether Jesus really was the Son of God or just a man imbued by his followers with that distinction, his crucifixion at the hands of the Romans bequeathed to Western culture a wholly new concept of affliction and deity. Christ nailed to the Cross abbreviated the equation that exists between creature-suffering and the Creator-God perhaps even more succinctly than the torturous relationship between the Israelites and Yahweh in the Old Testament. Where before God had been an "anxiety object" afflicting (or delivering) man from the "outside," in the Passion of Christ God's spirit put on the flesh, crept under our skin and located itself inside our very sensations of suffering. God dying on the Cross, God dying for our sins, was God saving us through His suffering. The revolution of thought that constituted the revelation of the New Testament was that God in his love suffers also.

If the God of the New Testament seems more kindly and compassionate toward mankind than the God of the Old Testament, this change is proportionate with the increase of Christ's sufferings at Golgotha — Place of a Skull. Affliction not only persists in the New Testament; it becomes the way to God. Nowhere, according to the logic of the crucifixion, are we more reconciled to the Lord than in Christ's passion. By becoming a man and suffering a human death, God sanctified suffering and redeemed it. No longer did suffering punitively correct a discrepancy between God's will and man's ways, but, rather, through the agony of Christ, it accented their reconciliation.[1] As the Catholic theologian Hans Küng put it:

> Nowhere did it become more clearly visible than in Jesus' life and work, suffering and death, that this God is a God for men, a God who is wholly on our side. He is not a theocratical God, creating fear, "from above," but a God friendly to men, *suffering with men*, "with us below." It is scarcely necessary to insist that we are talking here in metaphors, symbols, analogies. But what is meant is understandable enough and it is now clearer than ever that the God manifested in Jesus is not a cruel, despotic, legal-minded God, but a God encountering man as redeeming love, identifying himself in Jesus with suffering man.[2]

For the Christian, God can be known as a comfort that abides within affliction, a comfort that does not banish our sufferings but helps them to be borne. Through the agency of the crucified Christ, suffering becomes a meeting ground between God and man. It is not just that God approaches man by identifying with his sufferings; man moves nearer to God through suffering as well. Although pain and affliction may give rise to feelings of "being forsaken by God," from the Christian perspective it can "*become* the point of encounter with God,"[3] the point of our greatest intimacy with Him. As Paul wrote in his second letter to the Corinthians:

> Praise be to the God and Father of our Lord Jesus Christ, the Father of compassion and the God of all comfort, who comforts us in all our troubles, so that we can comfort those in any trouble with the comfort we ourselves have received from God. For just as the sufferings of Christ flow over into our lives, so also through Christ our comfort overflows. If we are distressed, it is for your comfort and salvation; if we are comforted, it is for your comfort, which produces in you patient endurance of the same sufferings we suffer. And our hope for you is firm, because we know that just as you share in our sufferings, so also you share in our comfort. (1:3–7)

"The Christian religion," writes Ludwig Feuerbach, "is the religion of suffering." [4] Through Christ's suffering and the mystical participation of our sufferings in his, profane man becomes Christian man. As Pascal said, "Suffering is the natural state of the Christian, just as health is that of the 'natural' man." [5] While human suffering circumscribes the finiteness of corporeal man, Christ's crucifixion and resurrection point the way which leads through suffering to the infinity of God. "The religious individual," according to Kierkegaard, "lies fettered in the finite with the absolute conception of God present to him in human frailty." [6] The smaller and more vulnerable each of us is, the greater and more transcending God seems. His strength is a function of our weakness, even as His limitlessness can be seen as a reversal of our puniness. If we would "seek first the kingdom of God (Matt. 6:33)," as the scripture demands, we must surrender ourselves first to our sufferings which, by transfixing us upon the cross of our own finiteness, eventually convey us into the presence of the infinite God, who, as *deus absconditus*, is paradoxically so very present in his absence.

Theology, the logic of deity, is a logic of suffering. Above all, the story of the risen Crucified provides a model of hanging in with affliction and pain until its *logos* emerges. Though we may feel utterly forsaken in a Gethsemane of meaningless despair, eventually a meaning will declare itself if we stay with what is happening. The incredible popularity of the Christian faith resides in the soul's need for examples such as the one Jesus provides. The soul that has been traumatized by events it cannot take in needs to be supplied with images that can hold the overwhelming events in a holding pattern until the imagination can respond to them. Without some kind of model of perseverance and endurance, the soul will tend to retreat from life into defensive withdrawal.

But there is a problem with the Christian model. Although the example of Christ crucified shepherds the soul through the shadowy valley of afflicting events, it does not take the soul through these events to *their* meanings. The Christian model of suffering belongs to the body of Christian meaning and returns all suffering to that body. Overwhelming events do not have value in themselves, only by virtue of God's having suffered them with us and only to the extent that they lead the soul to God. One meaning covers all events. No matter what it was that had transcended us, our suffering through it in Christ bears witness only to God's love for man as manifested by His sacrifice of His Son.

Here we do well to recall Nietzsche's critique of the Christian logic that would equate what is comforting to believe with what is actually true:

> How many people still make the inference: "one could not stand life if there were no God!" . . . — consequently there *must* be a God ! . . . what presumption to decree that all that is necessary for my preservation must also really *be there*! As if my preservation were anything necessary! [7]

Conjuring a God that is tailor-made to meet our needs for preservation does not help the soul to come to terms with the traumatic events that threaten to annihilate it. Indeed, when the soul is saved or rescued by this helpful deity, the events it was saved from may come to be viewed as even more traumatic. *Whatever we do not face but gain salvation from remains unredeemed and becomes Satanic. Evil is the excrement or waste product emitted by the salvation process itself. Ironically, the more we are saved, the more there is to be saved from.*

"No one comes to the Father but by the Son" (Matthew 11:27). This statement is more than a statement of the compassion of Christ; it is a statement of epistemology as well. No one comes to knowledge (i.e., the Father) except by suffering incomprehensible events with Christ through to the Christian truth that God is love. The circularity here is noteworthy: we start with the faith position that God manifests His love by suffering incomprehensible, overwhelming events with us and then decree that, though God is incomprehensible and overwhelming, His one great trait is the love He makes perfect with us in our suffering. But the irony remains that what we suffered on Good Friday is no clearer by Easter Monday. Indeed, the challenge of working out the unique epistemologies of what we had been suffering is then either forgotten altogether (repression) or attributed to the devil (splitting). By conveying the suffering soul to the monotheistic Father (before whom no other gods may be respected), the Christian model pre-empts the soul from suffering events through to the particular theophanies latent it them.

James Hillman has given considerable attention to a critique of the Christ model in his writings. He reminds us that *pathos*, the Greek root of our word "suffering," originally meant "'something that happens,' 'experiences,' being moved and the capacity to be moved."[8] In Hillman's view,

> The tremendous image of Christ dominates our culture's relation to pathologizing. The complexity of psychopathology with its rich variety of backgrounds has been absorbed by this one central image and been endowed with one main meaning: suffering. The *passio* of suffering Jesus — and it is as translation of Jesus' passion that "suffering" first enters our language — is fused with all experiences of pathology.[9]

Christ's model of suffering, in other words, has become the script for all suffering. Every event that is anomalous or dystonic to our ego's point of view is a place of crucifixion — abandonment (Gethsemane), agony (the whipping, the lance, the nails), humiliation (the crown of thorns), bitterness (the sop of vinegar), forgiveness ("Forgive them Father, they know not what they do"), and triumph over mortification (resurrection). As Hillman has put it,

> . . . Christianity has nailed suffering to resurrection — first nail: it is good for you; second nail; it is isolating and heroic, and third, it always leads to a better day, Easter. Well, it doesn't — we all know that! Suffering has other models, too, like deepening in the sense of Saturn, like dissolving and letting go in the sense of Dionysus, like raging and fighting back; it can make for prophesy; it can make for love; or the kinds of suffering we see in the women in Greek drama. We need many models, besides the Christian one, to locate our psychological experiences.[10]

Nothing in more crucial to the soul-making process, the process of turning events into experiences, than precision with regard to the events in question. Hillman's move of "bypass[ing] the Christian view by stepping behind it to the Greeks, to polytheism,"[11] frees psychology to experience events more in terms of their own aboriginal or archetypal backgrounds.

In the world of the ancient Greeks, a person who was ill or otherwise afflicted by transcending circumstances made a pilgrimage to Delphi and
asked the oracle there *which* gods or heroes he should sacrifice to in order
to get back into harmony with existence.

Sacrificing to a god within a pantheon of other gods is very different
than worshipping the so-called one true God. Where the monotheistic
God is at least as immense, transcending, and unabsorbable as the event
His Son has saved us from, a polytheistic god, by virtue of existing in a
pantheon, is a spirit of precise dimensions. Reflecting a trauma against
divine backgrounds within a polytheistic context does not preserve the
sense of its infinite and overwhelming proportions; rather, it divides or
differentiates this "infinity" in terms of a number of gods. Each particular
deity, simply by virtue of being different from the others, helps the sup-
plicant to particularize events while at the same time acknowledging that
they transcend him. When we know to which god an event belongs, we are
in a better place to individuate a relationship to it and incorporate it as an
experience. But until we go to the Delphi of a perspectival epistemology,
we remain in the radical monotheism of our trauma.

The God of love has not had much love for the other gods, as the
battles between Christians and pagans attest. As John Milton argues in
his nativity ode, when Christ was born, the oracles were stilled. No longer
could Delphi give us diagnosis. No longer could we find the altars specific to our afflictions and concerns. The process of returning events to
their archetypal dominants was expropriated by a single instance of it, the
Christian one. Incarnation, crucifixion, resurrection and apocalypse became our model of response for all events and happenings. The statement
"No one comes to the Father but by the Son," combined with the commandment that we have no other "as if" perspectives before God, became
the war cry of Christian soldiering. [12] Not only did it arm the Christian
against the pagan events that threatened him with harm; it armed him for
a counterattack. The Inquisition — the persecution of the heretics, the
alchemists, and the gnostics: the wholesale slaughter of the imagination
in the name of Christian truth — reveals the shadow side of the Christian
God of love and shows us the trauma that is constellated by the blood that
washes away all sin. [13]

In the Book of Revelation, the trauma of the triumphant Christ is made devastatingly clear. As a "wrathful Lamb" the Christ of the Apocalypse opens the seven seals of the "Book of Redemption," a book containing the story of man's fall through sin and rise through Christ (Heb. 2:5–9), and releases destruction upon the world in the form of war, famine, death, earthquake, solar eclipse, and the vengeance of the Christian martyrs (Rev. 6: 1–17). Though Christ may be the spirit who suffers with man and vicariously atones for man's sins, at the end, according to Christian orthodoxy, he will also visit affliction and cruelly and despotically judge those sins.

### Monotheism, Trauma, and the Failure of Calf-Making

The New Testament idea that God became incarnate in human flesh makes explicit the relationship that had always existed between what Shakespeare later referred to as "the thousand shocks which mortal flesh is heir to" and religion. Human pain had pointed to God long before Jesus suffered it. Whatever afflictions man was unable to reduce for himself became the act of a deity, the act of a god. In this way culture was engaged in a fashion helpful to the suffering individual. But when the suffering soul was unable to return its affliction to a *particular* deity, that affliction became the voice of the one true God.

The commandment of monotheism's God that man have no other gods before Him (Ex. 20:3) was the commandment of traumatic events which lay outside the capacity of mankind's present cultural containers to relativize and absorb. When Moses came down from Mount Sinai, his face burned pink from the presence of the Lord, the first commandment he read to his people from the list of ten was a "divine" admonishment that they have no other gods before His trauma.

The triumph of monotheism over polytheism — a triumph mistakenly viewed by many writers as culturally progressive — was the triumph of overwhelming events over the imagination. When events defy the imagination's capacity to differentiate between them, they assault the soul as a unified, monotheistic, omnipotent presence. Unable to make differences between itself and the huge jumble of events that assail it as its Other, the soul-making process becomes crippled. As Freud and Breuer put it, ". . . any impression which the nervous system has difficulty dealing with by means of associative thinking or by motor reaction becomes a psychical trauma."[14]

Let us imagine that the making of the covenant with the Trauma-God at Sinai was a defensive attempt to deny the felt sense of its already, in advance of itself, having been broken. While the biblical account holds that the children of Israel broke faith with the covenant *after* it was given to Moses, a psychoanalytic approach to the story would read this sequence in reverse. Regarded in this way, the making and un-making of the golden calf reflects the Israelites' failed attempt to master the events assailing them. Unable to form an imaginative relationship with those events, there remained no other recourse but to form a covenant with them. Monotheism, from this perspective, was less a triumph over polytheism than the failure of the imagination, the failure of soul-making. Man makes covenants with events in a monotheistic fashion only to the extent that they overwhelm his capacity to connect with them imaginatively — or, as Freud and Breuer said, through "associative thinking." Just as a psychic rupture precedes the phobic patient's compulsive propitiation of an aversive stimulus, so a breach in the psyche precedes the making of a covenant.

The notion that a covenant with God was broken by idolatrous acts of the imagination is the pious cover story of a consciousness identified with the trauma that the imagination had failed to protect it from. Indeed, it is only after our *calf* breaks that the omnipotent God, who accuses us of breaking our covenant with him, appears in the first place. At Sinai, the soul-making project that constituted the making of the golden calf was not enough to absorb the trauma, which the children of Israel faced. Unable to turn the events confronting them into experiences that could be reconciled with their existence, the victims blamed themselves, repented their attempts at mastery, and threw themselves upon the mercy of the events afflicting them as upon the mercy of a jealous, wrathful God.

## C.S. Lewis's Theodicy of Pain

"The great religions," writes C.S. Lewis, "were first preached, and long practiced, in a world without chloroform." [15] Affliction and suffering, Lewis rightly reminds us, has not been a discovery of modern science, but was ubiquitously present in the past as well, at the time when religions were being formed. Interestingly, Lewis uses this observation to suggest that pain was *not* the stimulus that elicited religion. "At all times," he writes, ". . . the inference from the course of events in this world to the goodness and wisdom of God would have been equally preposterous and it was never made." [16] This statement, of course, is highly dubious. Indeed, one need only skim through the Old Testament with a psychoanalytic eye to see that the wrath of God and His lovingkindness were complexly interconnected despite their ambiguity. And, yet, as if anticipating the present thesis that "God" and trauma operate in the psyche as overlapping categories, Lewis rules out from the beginning the role of the traumatic factor in the formation of religion. Seeking, perhaps, to counter the argument of some atheists that suffering is a proof of the non-existence of God (if God be defined as all-knowing, all-powerful, and benign), Lewis declares that it is only "*after* belief in God has been accepted [that] 'theodicies' explaining, or explaining away, the miseries of life, will naturally appear . . ." [17]

This statement, made in the early pages his book *The Problem of Pain*, supplies the fissure through which a deconstructive reading of his subsequent argument can be made. By ruling out the etiological significance of the phenomenon of pain in the creation of the God-concept, Lewis renders its significance stingingly present. The Trauma-God that Lewis brushes away so casually is as rudimentary to his argument — and, thus, as psychologically present within it — as the God that he goes on to affirm. Indeed, the theological slight-of-hand which Lewis employs to defer the problem of reconciling pain with a benevolent God until after we already believe in God's benevolence can be seen as a textbook example of how defenses such as splitting, rationalization, and idealization operate in a trauma-based faith.

Before quoting some of the more flamboyant examples of this clinical, and at the same time, theological syndrome from the pages of Lewis's theodicy of pain, we must note another of his slight-of-hand moves. In the chapter, "Human Pain," Lewis distinguishes between two groups of pain. The pain of group A Lewis describes as "a particular kind of sensation, probably conveyed by specialised nerve fibers, and recognizable by the patient as that kind of sensation whether he dislikes it or not (e.g., the faint ache in my limbs would be recognized as an ache even if I did not object to it.)" [18] The pain of group B Lewis describes as "any experience, whether physical or mental, which the patient dislikes." [19] Delineating the two groups of pain still more sharply, Lewis adds:

> It will be noticed that all Pains in sense A become Pains in sense B if they are raised above a certain very low level of intensity, but that Pains in B sense need not be Pains in A sense. Pain in the B sense, in fact, is synonymous with "suffering," "anguish," "tribulation," "adversity," or "trouble," and it is about it that the problem of pain arises. For the rest of this book Pain will be used in the B sense and will include all types of suffering: with the A sense we have no further concern. [20]

While Lewis's move here seems to be aimed at more intensely focusing attention upon the kind of pain most perturbing to the reader, his theodicean strategy, conscious or unconscious, is to place suffering in the arena of the likes and dislikes of the finite, egoistic human subject so that he can later make the argument that suffering is a divine corrective of man's merely finite and egoistic human perspective.

At first glance, even the psychoanalytically-minded reader may be seduced into accepting this punctuation of the problem. If neurosis is one-sidedness, as Jung said, [21] and if nothing is more foreign to the ego than the symptom, as Freud maintained, [22] then soul-making will require that the ego be re-made or re-imagined from the perspective of the symptoms which afflict us, as Hillman has suggested. [23] The pain of group B, which Lewis's God permits man to suffer, could, on this account, sometimes be therapeutic for man, even as for the psychoanalyst the ego can become more at home in the psyche by having it out with symptoms.

If we examine Lewis's argument more closely, however, we notice that the dichotomy into which he divides pain, while having a certain existential validity, is logically suspect with respect to the problem at hand. Since we are all used to ignoring the lesser aches and pains to which we are subject as a matter of course, we readily agree with Lewis to bracket from discussion those sensations of pain that have not reached an acute intensity. But precisely here is where a valence is surreptitiously shifted with respect to the larger question. The fact that we routinely pass over the minor aches and pains of our bodily life is merely an observation, not an argument. It does not entail our making philosophical divisions between types of pain, at least not on Lewis's scale. Theodicy cannot coast upon these coattails.

And yet, in Lewis's text it does. By dividing pain into his two types, the erstwhile apologist queers the pitch with respect to how the theological problem is put. Right off the bat, the *inhuman* face of pain drops out of the discussion, even while Lewis focuses our attention on "'suffering,' 'anguish,' 'tribulation,' 'adversity,' or 'trouble.'" We do not realize, perhaps Lewis does not realize, that he has maneuvered us into viewing the pain that is of concern to human beings as if man, through the agency of his likes and dislikes, were its measure. Though "all Pains in sense A become Pains in sense B if they are raised above a certain low level of intensity," we are advised that "with [pain in] the A sense we have no further concern." With this move, the logical level is collapsed into the literal, form into content. The fact that we do not merely suffer from this or from that, but may be "beside ourselves" with suffering, is no longer recognized. On the contrary, crammed into man as what Lewis calls "human pain," the pain that has produced this "beside-ourselves" state is denied its metaphysical status as man's Other. And it is in this way that man's ultimate Other, God, is defended in Lewis's text from the kind of critique that the problem of pain inspires.

But pain that exceeds the "certain low level of intensity" necessary for it to become a problem to man is not necessarily *bounded* by man. The grimace that contorts the face of a body racked with pain attests to the fact that the pain has passed beyond the limit of the body's capacity to measure or bear it — the likes and dislikes of the subject be damned! The cruel irony of pain, an irony Lewis neglects to square with his loving God, is that the very increase in intensity of pain that puts pain into the soul of man puts man out of his soul.

By way of contrast, let us think of Lewis's two kinds of pain in relation to the psychoanalytic concept of narcissism. Viewed from the perspective offered by this notion, Lewis's distinction may be read as a very weak charting of the territory Freud had in mind when he distinguished between primary and secondary narcissism — at least insofar as the pleasure principle is concerned. On this account, pains in Lewis's A sense would correspond, however dimly, to wounds at the level of primary narcissism. Denied by our character-defenses, pain inscribed at this early, infant-level may well seem as unobjectionable as Lewis suggests, but only because the repressed does not complain of its hurts in a direct manner! As for pain in Lewis's group B sense, this may be viewed as roughly corresponding to secondary narcissism, if only because it is louder, there being an ego present to raise objections to life's slings and arrows. But this does not mean that we may let the one level drop away, as Lewis would have us do. Streaming back to its source in the primary narcissism of the pre-verbal, body-self, a more articulate secondary narcissism may well pick up on the pains in A sense with a more differentiated sense of their acuteness. And further to this, analysis may reveal a veritable inferno of pre-verbal traumas, where before there had only been a faint ache in the limbs that was unobjectionable to the patient. Bringing back together what Lewis had defensively split apart in the course of his argument, we may here recall Winnicott's comment that even "the smallest skin lesion . . . concerns the whole personality . . ." [24]

We simply cannot let go the problem of pain in the group A sense as brashly as Lewis does, no matter how insignificant such aches and pains may seem. For to do so, as we have seen, undermines the metaphysical status of pain in general. Also, how the line is drawn between insignificant pain and full-blown suffering is far from clear when the unconscious is figured into the mix. In each case we must ask ourselves if this line is as clear as it appears to be or if, on the other hand, this is the point where defenses have been deployed. And then there is the issue of primary and secondary narcissism. Though there certainly are pains that are merely ego-dystonic

and attributable largely to man's narrow egoism, psychotic anxieties inscribed at the level of primary narcissism may lurk within these.

Here we must ask the question: could C.S. Lewis's God actually be
aversive stimulation that our traumatized being propitiates as wholly other
and calls by the name "Thou" precisely because it cannot be dealt with in
more immediately human terms? Is theodicy a defense, not of God but
from trauma?

The Scottish psychoanalyst Ronald Fairbairn described the theodicean or, as he calls it, "moral defense" that abused children utilize in
order to continue to hold the parents who have abused them in loving
esteem. Being dependent upon their parents, such children tend to develop the conviction that they themselves, and not their parents, are bad.
As Fairbairn explains:

> It is better to be a sinner in a world ruled by God than to live
> in a world ruled by the Devil. A sinner in a world ruled by God
> may be bad; but there is always a certain security to be derived
> from the fact that the world around is good — 'God's in His
> heaven — All's right with the world!'; and in any case there is al-
> ways the hope of redemption. In a world ruled by the Devil the
> individual may escape the badness of being a sinner; but he is
> bad because the world around him is bad. Further, he can have
> no sense of security and no hope of redemption. The only pros-
> pect is one of death and destruction. [24]

Let us now examine several of the morbid turns of argument Lewis
uses to reconcile pain and suffering with the existence of an omnipotent,
omniscient, and loving God.

> When our ancestors referred to pains and sorrows as God's 'ven-
> geance' upon sin they were not necessarily attributing evil passions to
> God; they may have been recognizing the good element in the idea of
> retribution. Until the evil man finds evil unmistakably present in his
> existence, in the form of pain, he is enclosed in illusion. Once pain has
> roused him, he knows that he is in some way or other 'up against' the
> real universe: he either rebels (with the possibility of a clearer issue and
> deeper repentance at some later stage) or else makes some attempt at
> an adjustment, which, if pursued, will lead him to religion. [25]

Despite the fact that he had earlier argued that man seeks to give an account of the connection between God and pain only after a benevolent God is already believed in, Lewis here describes a scenario where pain has been the springboard to recognition of God. In his elaboration of this point, Lewis describes this God-sent or God-permitted pain in benign terms as "God's megaphone":

> No doubt Pain as God's megaphone is a terrible instrument; it may lead to final and unrepented rebellion. But it gives the only opportunity the bad man can have for amendment. It removes the veil; it plants the flag of truth within the fortress of a rebel soul. [26]

Strategically, Lewis begins by looking at the function of pain for the bad man before he addresses the pain in the lives of those of us who do not behave in "bad" or "evil" ways. The implication so far is that God shows that He is a loving God by taking the trouble to speak through His megaphone of pain to those thick-skulled, sociopathic individuals who could hear His call in no other way. Since it is commonly believed that bad men need punishment in order to help them to become good, Lewis can most easily square pain with a loving God with reference to those cases where it is being suffered by morally reprehensible people. It is important to note here that it is as an extension of the bad man argument that Lewis, in the next paragraph, goes on to give his account of why bad things happen to good people.

> If the first and lowest operation of pain shatters the illusion that all is well, the second shatters the illusion that what we have, whether good or bad in itself, is our own and enough for us. Everyone has noticed how hard it is to turn our thoughts to God when everything is going well with us. We "have all we want" is a terrible saying when "all" does not include God. We find God an interruption. As St. Augustine says somewhere "God wants to give us something, but cannot, because our hands are full — there's nowhere for Him to put it." Or as a friend of mine said "we regard God as an airman regards his parachute; it's there for emergencies but he hopes he'll never have to use it."

Now God, who has made us, knows what we are and that our happiness lies in Him. Yet we will not seek it in Him as long as He leaves us any other resort where it can even plausibly be looked for. While what we call "our own life" remains agreeable we will not surrender it to Him. What then can God do in our interests but make "our own life" less agreeable to us, and take away the plausible sources of false happiness? It is just here, where God's providence seems at first to be most cruel, that the Divine humility, the stooping down of the Highest, most deserves praise. [27]

Compared to God — who is the all-good, all-powerful, absolute truth — we, like the bad man, are all to some extent off the track. If painful events afflict us, if our worldly hopes go bankrupt or tragedy strikes one of our loved ones, God is at work, recalling us to Himself through His divine megaphone. After all, man cannot live by bread alone, and famine can be squared with the love of God by seeing it as God's attempt to lead us to His spirit, which is our proper food. The things of the world are merely relative; God is eternal. By calling to us in our pain, God reminds us of this distinction, enabling us to surrender to the absolute. But from the psycho-analytic perspective, events from the so-called "merely relative" world that are traumatic and overwhelming cannot be relativized by the soul (which they have punctured) for they seem to the soul to be no less absolute than the so-called one true God. If it is a traumatic or painful event, which has conveyed the soul to a religious experience, how can we be sure whether that soul is surrendering to the ontological God of religion and theology or simply to a bad object, interior saboteur, or superego representation, which has been abstracted from the severity of the hurt itself?

At the end of this argument, it is interesting to note the ruse Lewis uses to repress a psychological reading of the relationship between pain and religious conversion. Rather than entertain the prospect that we defend ourselves from overwhelming events by deifying them and identifying with them (Anna Freud called this mode of defense "identification with the aggressor"), Lewis simply acts this out in a sermonizing manner:

If God were proud He would hardly have us on such terms: but He is not proud, He stoops to conquer, He will have us even though we have shown that we prefer everything else to Him, and come to Him because there is "nothing better" now to be had. The same humility is shown by all those Divine appeals to our fears which trouble high-minded readers of scripture. It is hardly complimentary to God that we should choose Him as an alternative to Hell: yet even this He accepts. [29]

That we come to God in our pain Lewis sees as evidence of how truly great and unconditional God's love for us is. The traumatic thought that God might be identical to the very trauma we are fleeing, a thought that almost leaps off the page, is repressed by Lewis as he flees it to a now re-doubled affirmation of the love of God made manifest in pain.

I cannot say whether Lewis's argument is good theology or not. It has had great popular success. It can be read, however, through psychological eyes, as a vivid example of how such Freudian revenants as splitting, rationalization, identification with the aggressor and idealization can work together towards a deification of suffering.

Masochism and Mysticism

On a cold winter night, in what was by no means an isolated incident, a fourteenth-century Catholic monk

> shut himself up in his cell . . . stripped himself naked . . . and took his scourge with the sharp spikes, and beat himself on the body and on the arms and legs, till blood poured off him as from a man who has been cupped. One of the spikes of the scourge was bent crooked, like a hook, and whatever flesh it caught it tore off. He beat himself so hard that the scourge broke into three bits and the points flew against the wall. He stood there bleeding and gazed at himself. It was such a wretched sight that he was reminded in many ways of the appearance of the beloved Christ when he was fearfully beaten. Out of pity for himself he began to weep bitterly. And he knelt down, naked and covered in blood in the frosty air, and prayed to God to wipe out his sins from before his gentle eyes. [30]

Given the soul's natural tendency to divinize and propitiate all hurts and pains it is unable to handle through "associative thinking or motor reaction," we should not be surprised to find masochistic suffering playing a central role in the lives of persons who have intentionally sought encounter with God. In order to enhance their relationship to God, mystics, saints, and martyrs have long exploited the physiological relationship between suffering and spirituality by intentionally subjecting themselves to pain and affliction. Just as the divinely victimized Job shrieked out in his torments, "Even after my skin is destroyed, Yet from my flesh I shall see God (Job 19:26)," many religious seekers have attempted to awaken the gift of mystic vision in themselves by deliberately destroying their flesh through self-mortifying acts.

The more we are hurt, the more we are beside ourselves with pain, the closer we are to ecstatic union with that overwhelming intensity of stimulus the pious have called God. While low levels of pain may make us peevish and personal, intolerable affliction destroys the self, releasing the sufferer from the finite limits personhood had imposed. As Karen Horney writes, ". . . all masochistic strivings are ultimately directed toward satisfaction, namely, toward the goal of oblivion, of getting rid of self with all its conflicts and all its limitations." [31]

In the annihilation of the soul's capacity to make experiences, the mystic "experiences" divine rapture. As the intensity of a pain grows greater and greater, it eventually surpasses the capacity of the imagination to accommodate it. [32] Consciousness shatters. Metaphors give way to symbols. Held in thrall by the flaming nerves that burn in the tortured body, the traumatized soul surrenders its imaginal freedom and prostrates itself before the fire of the body's agony as before a vision of the Lord. What had begun simply enough as the painful sensations of self-torture becomes in an instant — precisely that instant in which the agony is intensive enough to estrange the soul from the body — the symbolism of a transcending spirituality. "I could not possibly explain it," writes St. Theresa of Avila,

> In his hands I saw a great golden spear, and at the iron tip there appeared to be a point of fire. This he plunged into my heart several times so that it penetrated to my entrails. When he pulled it out, I felt that he took them with it, and left me utterly

consumed by the great love of God. The pain was so severe that it made me utter several moans. The sweetness caused by this intense pain is so extreme that one cannot possibly wish it to cease, nor is one's soul then content with anything but God. [33]

The way of the mystic is the way of affliction. By inflicting pain upon herself, the mystic intensifies the "profound dis-harmony between the sense-world and the human self" [34] until the physical world feels completely inhospitable and her desirous body "creates / From its own wreck the thing it contemplates . . ." [35]

Although the New Testament does not specifically instruct the Christian soul to torture itself, it states quite clearly that the path of the Christian is a path that leads through suffering. "Through many tribulations," the Apostles told new initiates, "we must enter the kingdom of God" (Acts 24:22). "Behold," Jesus told his followers, "I have given you authority to tread upon serpents and scorpions . . . nothing will hurt you" (Luke 10:19). Paul is particularly clear on this point, "boasting" of his own afflictions (2 Cor. 11:23–33) as if these were the humbling prerequisites to the "visions and revelations of the Lord" he had been subject to (2 Cor. 12:1–10). In the same passage, Paul tells his Corinthian audience that he suffered "a thorn in the flesh, a messenger of Satan to buffet me — to keep me from exalting myself" because of "the surpassing greatness of the revelations." Despite three appeals to God for healing, Paul writes, his malady persisted. Nevertheless, the great apostle suffered his thorn gladly for the Lord told him, "My grace is sufficient for you, for power is perfected in weakness." Writing in a similar vein, Peter, in this first epistle, suggests that our spiritualization is directly proportionate with our sufferings: ". . . to the degree that you share the sufferings of Christ, keep rejoicing; so that also at the revelation of His glory, you may rejoice with exultation" (1 Peter 4:13).

Just as crucifixion was followed by resurrection in the life of Christ, some mystics have attempted to partake in the pleasures of Christ's risen life by following "the Way of the Cross" through whatever sorrows and humiliations they can subject themselves to. [36] As the fourteenth-century mystic John Tauler explains in his "Second Sermon for Easter Day":

> A great life makes reply to him who dies in earnest even in the least of things, a life which strengthens him immediately to die

a greater death; a death so long and strong, that it seems to him hereafter more joyful, good and pleasant to die than to live, for he finds life in death and light shining in darkness. [37]

Suffering, in the words of Thomas à Kempis, author of the classic text of Catholic devotional *De Imitatione Christi*, is the "gymnastic of eternity," the "terrible initiative caress of God." While mostly the soul flees pain as if it were fleeing the wrath of God, it can also deify traumatic stimulation by willingly impaling itself upon it like the saints, mystics and martyrs who run so "eagerly and merrily to the Cross." Just as God is encountered in pestilence and death, famine and flood, earthquake and lightning flash, He is encountered as well in the sting of the scourge with which one assaults one's own body. Through acts of masochism, the seeker of God can invoke the loving sadism of his Lord's touch. Marx was right: religion *is* the opium of the people. With the same firing of nervous impulses that the flagellant brings about to invoke God, he releases the natural opiates in his afflicted body. God is the leather strap, the willow switch, the cat-o'-nine-tails, and the cane. He is the gnashing of the teeth, the raving of the nerves, and the creature's anguished cry. No matter how we are flayed, cut, broken, or pierced — voluntarily or involuntarily — we encounter God in trauma.

## Do Not Take My Name In Vain

In his book *The Idea of the Holy*, Rudolf Otto speculates that the earliest names for deity were derived from the inarticulate shrieks and cries which were emitted from the larynx of early man when he shuttered in terror and amazement before overwhelmingly numinous events. Quoting from the Kena-Upanishad, Otto shows how involuntary sounds that express the numinous feelings stirring in man when he encounters overwhelming events (such as thunder and lightning) may have become associated with the Numinous itself,

> This is the way It (sc. Brahman) is to be illustrated:
> When the lightnings have been loosened:
> Aaah!

When that has made the eyes be closed —
Aaah! —
So far concerning Deity (*devata*). [38]

If Otto is correct, if the earliest names man gave to deity corre-
sponded to the gasps and cries of his startled, frightened creaturehood,
the commandment that we not take the name of the Lord in vain (Ex.
20:7) is tantamount to a commandment that we cover our mouths, split
off our reactions to what has hurt or frightened us, and reverence it
with silence.

I flailed my fists at nothing,
And yet I was defeated.
My soul of itself did tire,
And I longed for the dust to claim me.
But when a groan interrupted by dying,
I glimpsed a strange justice dependent upon
The merciless turning of the world. [39]

When the soul tires of itself and words fail, when metaphors can
no longer be found through which to individuate a relationship to transcending events, a groan may be emitted, a groan so different from the
soul's usual experience of itself that, as Paul would later say, it seems to
be "not I who speak, but Him in me." By prohibiting the invectives of
the traumatized soul, the commandment not to take the name of the
Lord in vain deprives it of its most natural mechanism for anxiety release. Presumably, if we could utter a shriek or a moan these could be
used to differentiate overwhelming experiences at least to a minimal degree. Were the soul permitted to hear the difference between one groan
and another, the differences in intensity, pitch and timbre, it could use
these sounds as metaphors to particularize the events which overwhelm
it. But the commandment not to cry out forbids the comparison of inarticulate sounds, preserving the awesomeness of the eliciting stimulus
and traumatic response. With each cry that is held back in the throat,
the event to which it was a response becomes more and more other until, like a God, it becomes wholly other. God is the deferral of cursing
and swearing, the deferral of groaning, weeping, howling and shrieking,

and the indefinite postponement of whimpering in the dark. He is the inarticulate made Holy, the sanctification of the literally unspeakable, a circumcised tongue.

Of course, the commandment not to take the name of the Lord in vain is also a commandment not to swear false covenants. When men made covenants or contracts with one another they solemnized them by swearing before the presence of God. "If I default on my agreement with you, may the Lord strike me dead with lightning." Ironically, the overwhelming and unpredictable events with which early man made covenants in order to render them less traumatic and less unpredictable became the background in whose terms he attempted to render his secular affairs more benign and predictable. Agreements made with reference to the name of God were made with reference to that jumble of traumatic events before which man trembled when he uttered the inarticulate sounds from which the deity's name was later derived. God is as severe as the events that took our speech away, replacing it with the cries and groans of a traumatized creaturehood. "If I break my agreement with you, may God subject me to the moaning and groaning of the sufferings which mankind has attempted to propitiate by splitting off and deifying."

Words, as the saying goes, are cheap. In order to make them binding and substantive, early man linked them to the inarticulate shrieks and moans through which he submitted to the authority of overwhelming stimulation as if before a God. Even today, words may seem more credible if there is a plaintiveness in them, an inarticulate excess of emotion. And, yet, like a confession at gun-point, trauma-laden speech may give us cause for skepticism. Its sincerity may be entirely a function of its identification with the power that has transcended, hurt, startled or frightened it.

In the New Testament, Jesus, God's suffering son, is called "the Word" and described as being linguistically pre-existent in God. "In the beginning there was the Word, and the Word was with God, and the Word was God" (John 1:1). Perhaps, this Christic Word which dwelt from the beginning with God and which later "became flesh" (John 1:14) was actually the pathetic groan or inarticulate whimper of early man — not a word at all but, rather, the failure of words, an anti-word. No one comes to the father but by the shrieks and groans of His Son, the "living Word." Christ groaning on the cross, Christ groaning *with* us, is Christ groaning vicariously *for* us.

If, as T.S. Eliot wrote, the world will end "not with a bang but a whimper," perhaps it will be with the whimpers we have "given to the Lord." If, today, "we are hollow men," perhaps it is because throughout our yesterdays we have devalued ourselves through monotheism. After several millennia of our endowing overwhelming events with the incarnational vulnerability they make so unbearable in ourselves, the whimpering of our displaced humanity has probably reached the mega-tonnage sufficient to break forth with quite a bang. On the other hand, if each of us, individually, would allow ourselves to whimper — to whimper and curse, and curse and swear — perhaps we could begin to diffuse the stock-pile of insufficiently experienced events and emotions that we have given to the Lord and learned to call "God."

## *Sacrificium Intellectus* and the One True God

"If God is small enough for me to understand Him, then He's not big enough to be God!" says the Believer with a blink. Perhaps no popular adage could better express how the no-name God of monotheistic religion produces unconsciousness. The adage not only displays a mind-set for which the will to believe has upstaged the will to understand, it displays a predilection for believing *big*. "If you're going to believe, believe BIG!," the believer ostentatiously booms. Ironically, while monotheistic religion boasts that its God is larger than what its understanding can encompass, His size does not exceed the immensity of the credulity it demonstrates with this boasting. Perhaps large monotheistic Gods are not exclusively the consequence of huge tribulations, but are the consequence of big believers as well. Indeed, what would become of the one true God, the jealous God before whom one may recognize no other categories of understanding, if He did not have big believers to sustain and promote Him?

Traumatic events are not all painful. Frequently, the imagination is fixated by events, which stop it from imagining on but do not cause pain.

The birth of a child, for instance, may be as overwhelming for the new father as for the mother. The sudden appearance of the new life immediately cancels the conventions of its parents' old life, temporarily bankrupting their previous soul-making. We should not be surprised, therefore, that new parents often admit to being afraid of their children and sometimes even suffer depression or psychosis following a birth they may have joyously anticipated. It is a tremendous responsibility to be the parent of an overwhelming event, the mother or father of God.

But even events that are neither painful nor as overwhelming as the "miracle of childbirth" can stop the imagination when they are taken to be subject to the will of a divine being whom by definition we cannot understand. If God would not be God if He were small enough for man to understand, and if God is working in mysterious ways in events that defy man's comprehension, it would be hubris for men and women to try to bring clarity to life through the action of their own minds. The more we hold to be accounted for by an explanatory category which we do not understand, the more we fail to grapple with the inherent mystery of the events themselves. The idea that God is absolutely beyond man's capacity to fathom dislocates the mediating function of the imagination, devaluing the metaphors and models it creates as merely the productions of a finite intelligence. But when the soul-making process is devalued, the psyche itself is at risk. The soul-destroying consequence of worshipping a God who is identical with our inability to understand Him is that we then tend to propitiate, as if they too were completely transcending, events that the soul might otherwise have been able to comprehend and absorb.

It is not only as the defensive maneuver of an exhausted imagination that the God-concept appears and produces unconsciousness. Unconsciousness is built right into the notion of an omniscient God. Inasmuch as we "explain" what we cannot understand by dropping the name of a God we hold to be at least as inexplicable, we have merely glorified darkness as mystery. The unfathomable mind of God is an anti-concept which clarifies nothing. It is not just that the less we can explain the more omniscient we believe God to be. The corollary is also true: the more omniscient God seems to be, the less we even attempt to make comprehensible for ourselves.

What happens to events when we try to come to terms with them by appealing to the God whose claim to divinity resides in his being bigger than what we can understand? More: what happens to our *relationship* with events we cannot yet comprehend when we attempt to comprehend them in terms of a God whose omniscience is a function of the *sacrificium intellectus* we make when turning to Him?

Even when we leave quite to one side references to the wrath of God and stress, as does our loud believer, that He works in mysterious ways which are ultimately loving and benign, the God-concept can have a traumatizing effect upon the psyche. *Whenever the core category of our epistemology is a divine category whose ways are inscrutable and mysterious, the overwhelming quality of the events we refer to it is preserved.* The less we can make sense of our world, the more omniscient God seems. The more unable we are to make a residence for ourselves in the world, the more we seem to rest in Him.

The God before whom one may have no other forms of knowing is a disturbed metaphor. While it moves in the psyche among other metaphors, it is a metaphor that denies its relativity as a metaphor. Obsessive-compulsive, monomaniacal, paranoid: the monotheistic God-image is the presiding deity over many clinical syndromes. In order to remain psychological, the psyche must not only relativize the material and social events that overwhelm it, but the ideological and religious ones as well. And, of course, first among these is the One who must always be first, the One who commands us to know Him as the one true God.

Metaphysical Conjectures

"God is a conjecture," wrote Nietzsche in *Thus Spoke Zarathustra*, "but I desire that your conjectures should not reach beyond your creative will."[40] In Nietzsche's view, it is as wrong-headed as it is wrong-spirited to worship a metaphysical object, an object that is beyond the scope of the culture which we as culture-makers are creating. To do so is only to worship a projected, reified, hypostatized version of the existential issues we have been unable to confront and absorb. The Creator-god which men conjecture is inversely proportionate to their creative responses to the challenges of existence. The paler a people's response, the more bloated has become their God with projected creativity. By declaring the death of God, Nietzsche sought to release again into human hands the creativity that man had displaced into the Godhead. God, in Nietzsche's view, did not make Adam out of clay during the second week of an original creation; rather, men fashioned God out of clay, erased their fingerprints, and then blew the graven idol into supernatural proportions by means of abnegations of the will.

But why is man so quick to hide his creative power in a metaphysical conjecture, a metaphysical conceit? Perhaps it is because necessity, the mother of invention, is not appeased by our creative efforts, but again and again snarls our path with obstacles and troubles. While civilization has solved many human problems, there are other problems which have proved insoluble. As Shelley put it, if it were not for the "clogs" of "chance, and death, and mutability," the imagination of man "might oversoar / The loftiest star of unascended heaven, / Pinnacled dim in the intense inane."[41] Unable to exhaust the contingencies that drive us to create with our inventions, we eventually abdicate our creative power and reside conflict-free in the state of grace that accompanies the projection of our creative power, the abnegation of our will. But residing in grace is like living on credit. Sooner or later our account comes due, and we find ourselves irredeemably overdrawn. So bankrupt have we become by the worship of our old God that we require a new God to bail us out.

Just as we conjecture a creation to end all creation, a God to end all Gods, now we require a sacrifice to end all sacrifices. We require a vicarious atonement, a new testament to balance the vicarious displacements of the old testament. Unable to create our way out or through the traumatic level of existence, we conjecture a way out beyond the reach of our creating will. When this also breaks down and the trauma ("chance, death, and mutability") confronts us again, we try to patch up the cracks in our theological defenses by packing the trauma off on the scapegoat's back with the notion of an only begotten Son who takes the sins and pains of the world onto his shoulders and suffers them all for us.

## The Puer and the Intense Inane

In *Prometheus Unbound,* Shelley describes the religious sensibility of the puer-gripped ego. Jupiter, the Father-god, has been ousted from his throne and Man's imagination is freed from the limits, which he, as divine artificer, had set for it. The situation is Nietzschean: God is dead and man, but for the frailty of his mortal existence, is omnipotent in his creative power.

> but man:
> Passionless? no: yet free from guilt or pain,
> Which were, for his will made or suffered them,
> Nor yet exempt, though ruling them like slaves,
> From chance, and death, and mutability,
> The clogs of that which else might oversoar
> The loftiest star of unascended heaven,
> Pinnacled dim in the intense inane. [42]

The intense inane, like the Lacanian Real, is as traumatically numinous as it is unmediated. Standing by the sea, the usual horizon line obliterated by fog, we experience the divine influx of what before had been "out there." Peering into the nothingness of mist and fog, minute molecules of possible thoughts boil in the featureless presence that churns before our eyes and the silence thick about us occultly hums.

Whenever the "doors of perception" are flung open onto nothing, the numinosity of the archetypes that our absent objects would have insulated us from — had they in fact been there — knocks at the door of our creative power. Opening the door we find the stoop empty, but intensely inane. Like the sea at our ear in a seashell, decontextualized into an inane mystery, the blood of emptiness and silence is the absent God transsubstantiating Himself in our minds. Knowing no God, but yet, deeply stirred by His absence, one feels that one could create anything. With Nietzsche we ask ourselves,

> Who gave us the sponge to wipe away the whole horizon? What
> did we do when we loosened the earth from its sun? Whither

does it now move? Whither do we move? Away from all suns? . . .
Do we not stray, as through infinite nothingness? Does not the
empty space breathe upon us? . . . Does not night come on con-
tinually, darker and darker? Shall we not have to light lanterns
in the morning? [43]

Whenever a sacral form splits — be it a theological dogma, a scientific
theory, a politic of experience, or a social role — it splits like an atom. The
imagination explodes. Possibilities inflate the ego, and the puer flies.

Shelley suggests in his poem that the traumatic contingencies of
chance and death and mutability are the only checks on our otherwise omnipotent imaginations. However, the opposite is also true. It is precisely
through these limits and conditions that the intense inane breaks through.
Wherever there is a gap in the human sphere, a window festers open in the
soul. A neurotic symptom, an absent parent, the deficiencies of a modern
education — all arrow longings that would, but for our still living, unin-
fected parts, "oversoar the loftiest star . . ."

Likewise, in our times of indecision, we may find that we hover
in the intense inane, reluctant to incarnate into either side of the
choice conflicting us. By remaining undecided (or putting this more
positively, by tolerating ambivalence), we live in a sort of subtle body,
unbounded by the clogs to which decisiveness would fix us. From one
point of view, we are un-born, living provisionally, in need of "grounding," typically puer, or traumatized right out of our bodies. From another, it is as if we were in the bardo realm which in Tibetan tradition
is the realm between death and rebirth. In Tibetan tradition the priest,
reading from a guide book describing post-mortem states of the soul,
counsels the dead on the importance of staying in the bardo as long
as possible, lest one's craving for incarnation lead one to take on an
inferior form through premature rebirth. In our indecision, perhaps,
we are being this same priest with respect to our culture's dead God.
Hölderlin, Heidegger, Rilke, and Jung all characterized our times as
impoverished or needy times. By this they meant that we live in the
anxiety-ridden gap between the God that has passed away, and the
God, if such He will be, who is to come. Bootstrapping these ideas and
traditions together (Jung spoke of amplification), we are inspired to

ask the spiritual question: what if we could ascend the loftiest star and find our standing there?

Hubris? Certainly. But there is a sense in which our symptoms, vulnerability, and decay — all that we are subject to *postmortem dei* — re-baptizes us in the intense inane. And it is precisely through such baptized breakdowns that culture is reborn.

### Schizoid Defenses

Trauma is the body of the world and the body of man. "Chance, and death, and mutability" are our existential lot. To defend himself from the ontological insecurity of his existence, man has developed schizoid defenses. To use Laing's terminology, the self has been divided. The self splits off from the body and hovers above it — a false self. World becomes mere worldliness, and a transcendental, heavenly world is split off and affirmed.

> The self, as long as it is "uncommitted to the objective element," is free to dream and imagine anything. Without reference to the objective element it can be all things to itself — it has unconditioned freedom, power, creativity. But its freedom and its omnipotence are exercised in a vacuum and its creativity is only the capacity to produce phantoms. The *inner honesty, freedom, omnipotence, and creativity*, which the "inner" self cherishes as its ideals, are cancelled, therefore, by a co-existing tortured sense of self-duplicity, of the lack of any real freedom, of utter impotence and sterility. [44]

As the self grows bigger and bigger in its disembodied vacuum, as God grows bigger and bigger in His world-transcending vacuum, larger and larger traumatic experiences are required to bring the consciousness that has split off into the false-self and God back into touch with the body of the world and man. The traumatic events we deny return to us cumulatively. At the end of millennia there are indeed judgment days, days of reckoning. The bigger God becomes, the more events we channel off into the void of his righteousness, love, and grace, the more perilous becomes the human situation. And God does become bigger:

> The schizoid defense against "reality" has, however, the grave disadvantage that it tends to perpetuate and potentiate the original threatening quality of reality.[45]

Mountains get made out of avoided molehills, and then, ironically, the molehills of a millennium of denial *do* sum up to mountains. In order to feel anything in our aloof vacuum, there must be huge explosions. In order to break through our catatonic withdrawal, there must be shock treatments. When man created God, he created the Auschwitz oven. The flaming fire-pot that Abraham saw in his dream of the ceremony of the covenant with Yahweh returns in the demonic guise of Hitler's final solution. In order for us to feel anything, 6 million people had to be exterminated. The last century has enacted a Derridean deconstruction of our civilization's logo-centric, Judeo-Christian defense, the Judeo-Christian covenant. In the text of history we can read the subtext of God, the horror of the Great Code. God is the oven. God is the atom bomb. God is a trauma.

Don't Touch!

The finger burned on the hot stove supplies the decision to avoid the repetition of a similar event in the future. "Once burned, twice shy," goes the popular adage. The relationship that develops between the singed finger and the aversive object — in this case the kitchen stove — is based upon mis-trust. The burned finger comes to respect the hot stove, to reverence and propitiate it. The reflex withdrawing the burned finger, the finger's pained response, is an act of piety before the glowing element, an act of prostration before the stimulus, the stove. Pentecost: recoiling from its experience of the stove-God, the finger stiffens and throbs, slayed in the spirit. Prayers are offered; devotions are observed; oven-mitts and priestly robes are worn. In the rhetoric of trust, supplications are made to the object of our mistrust: "Lord have mercy upon us." "Forgive us our trespasses." "Lead us not into temptation [trauma], but deliver us from evil [pain]." In order to protect ourselves from what has hurt us, we white-wash it and identify with it. Our trauma is converted into a loving father, and our mis-trust hypocritically refined into a covenantal relationship with Him. Religion originates at our fingertips.

## Incarnation and the Bomb

What is pathological about incarnational thinking is that it is exaggerated in two directions at once. Both in its idealism and in its pragmatism it goes too far. The incarnational mind imagines in terms of ultimate inventions and fi-nal solutions. Its logic is a logic of God becoming man and of man becoming God. Its fascination is with a sacrifice to end all sacrifice, a "once and for all" solution. What the incarnational perspective reckons to be spirit it must ren-der in the flesh. The proof is in the pudding. Just ask the Japanese. They have become experts on incarnation — American-pragmatist style. They study it, replicate it, and industrialize it, because they are fixated in the trauma of it. (Identification with the aggressor is the specific defense mechanism.) The Americans so loved the world and peace that they nuked the Japanese for its redemption. Truman justified the atomic bomb as the necessary violence in a war that would end all war. No more pistols and grenades. No more eye for an eye, tooth for a tooth, Old Testament combat. It's the New Testament now. Now we will call into being a new order. Now we will destroy whole cit-ies with our Savior-bombs. After all, isn't that the mystery: they have to lose their lives to gain them, in a higher form, redeemed?

## The Martyrdom of Táhirih

God is a trauma, the sum of the pains, problems and catastrophes we have been unable to absorb into creative responses. The name "God" is the x-value we assign to events that are to hot to handle, too big, too numinous, too unknown. Religion, likewise, is a form of divine arithmetic, an algebra of propitiation.

The end of religion, theoretically, would correspond to the absorption of its traumatic contents and iconographic substitutes into man's ongoing creative process, into soul. At the apocalyptic end of a millennium, the trauma which has been displaced into the extra-human world of spiritual conjectures erupts. We pass beyond our eschatology, beyond our conjectures, beyond the orienting structures of our fear. The world comes to an end. Usually, this ending is conceived of moralistically as a judgement day. On the one hand, a trauma-free heaven is imagined for those who have piously propitiated the trauma; on the other hand, a traumatic hell is imagined for those who have not worshipped the trauma. Clearly, this moralistic mythology of the final absorption of trauma is the expression of a consciousness still very much propitiating of trauma.

In the Book of Revelation, the triumphant assimilation of trauma is imagined as the marriage of Christ and the city, New Jerusalem, which descends out of heaven as a Bride adorned to meet the Bridegroom. In this marriage the incest taboo is finally lifted, and we are to enter a new dispensation, one entirely different from the Old Testament totem and taboo.

In our culture, in most cultures, women have been associated with what Jung called "earth, darkness, the abysmal side of the bodily man with his animal passions and instinctual nature and to 'matter' in general." [46] While men have tended to be regarded as rational spirits, women have tended to be seen as irrational, inferior, and weak. Whether as Lilith, Eve, Pandora, Whore of Babylon, witch at the stake, hysteric in Charcot's clinic or on Freud's couch, woman has been imagined to be either trauma itself or particularly susceptible to it.

Like everything else that is associated with trauma, woman is split in two. Just as we conjecture about traumatic events in terms of pain and pleasure, good and bad, positive and negative, heaven and hell, we split the feminine into a virgin and a whore. Whether we look east to the Arab countries where women are covered from head to toe, or west to America where women are more scantily clad, the whore-madonna complex is everywhere present.

But what does all this look like at the end of a millennium of prohibi-
tions and propitiations? What does it look like when the traumatic contents of a culture shed the trappings of misogynist repression and stand
before that culture as a bride before her husband?

In 1848, in the Persian hamlet of Bada<u>sh</u>t, Baha'u'lláh, prophet and
founding father of the Bahá'í religion, gathered eighty-one followers
around him and revealed to them daily a new dispensation from the old
Islamic law.

> Each day of that memorable gathering witnessed the abroga-
> tion of a . . . law and the repudiation of a long-established tradi-
> tion. The veils that guarded the sanctity of the ordinances of
> Islám were sternly rent asunder, and the idols that had so long
> claimed the adoration of their blind worshippers were rudely
> demolished. [47]

The conference at Bada<u>sh</u>t was similar in a sense to Christ's Sermon
on the Mount. Bahá'u'lláh's daily abrogation of a traditional Islamic law
was intended to inaugurate a new aeon, even as Christ sought to inaugurate a new aeon by giving the old Jewish laws a new twist: "You have heard
that the ancients were told . . . But I say unto you that . . ." Bahá'u'lláh,
doubtless, saw his law-breaking as the fulfilment of the orthodox tradition.
Like Christ, he had not come "to abolish the Law or the Prophets, but to
fulfil [them]" (Matthew 5:17–18).

The key difference between the Sermon on the Mount and the
Conference at Bada<u>sh</u>t was that while Christ's revision of the law was given
to prepare man for the *coming* of the end of the world and the Kingdom
of God, Bahá'u'lláh's law-breaking was an attempt to help man to take up
residence in a world that had already ended, a kingdom that, in the revelation of the *Báb* (or Gate), had already come. If the situation during Christ's
time was pre-apocalyptic (as presumably it still is for the Judeo-Christian
world), the situation for the followers of the *Báb* was apocalyptic right at
the very time of the Bada<u>sh</u>t conference. Perhaps what happened next at
Bada<u>sh</u>t can be accounted for in terms of the apocalyptic intensity that the
conference was invested with, a traumatic intensity for which not everyone
present was ready.

During the conference, the famous female follower of the *Báb,* Táhirih,
was reproached by her more conservative fellow-disciples for transgressing
the time honored traditions of Islamic law. The issue came to a head when
Táhirih appeared before her fellow disciples unveiled.

> Consternation immediately seized the entire gathering. All
> stood aghast before this sudden and most unexpected appari-
> tion. To behold her face unveiled was to them inconceivable.
> Even to gaze at her shadow was a thing which they deemed im-
> proper, inasmuch as they regarded her as the very incarnation of
> Fátimih [the daughter of Muhammad], the noblest emblem of
> chastity in their eyes.
>
> Quietly, silently, and with the utmost dignity, Táhirih stepped
> forward and, advancing towards Quddús, seated herself on his
> right-hand side. Her unruffled serenity sharply contrasted with
> the affrighted countenances of those who were gazing upon
> her face. Fear, anger, and bewilderment stirred the depths of
> their souls. That sudden revelation seemed to have stunned
> their faculties. Abdu'l-Kháliq-i-Lsfáhani was so gravely shaken
> that he cut his throat with his own hands. Covered with blood
> and shrieking with excitement, he fled away from the face of
> Táhirih. A few, following his example, abandoned their com-
> panions and forsook their Faith. A number were seen standing
> speechless before her, confounded with wonder.
>
> . . . A feeling of joy and triumph had now illumined her face.
> She rose from her seat and, undeterred by the tumult that she
> had raised in the hearts of her companions, began to address
> the remnant of that assembly. Without the least premeditation,
> and in language that bore a striking resemblance to that of the
> Qur'án, she delivered her appeal with matchless eloquence and
> profound fervour. She concluded her address with this verse of
> the Qur'án: "Verily, amid gardens and rivers shall the pious
> dwell in the seat of truth, in the presence of the potent King."
>
> . . . [Concluding her address, Táhirih declared:] "This day
> is the day of festivity and universal rejoicing . . . the day on
> which the fetters of the past are burst asunder. Let those who
> have shared in this great achievement arise and embrace each
> other.'" [48]

Unfortunately, the trauma that was released with the unveiling of Táhirih's face was not absorbed into the spirit that her eloquent assurances sought to inaugerate. Following the Badasht conference were years of persecution and martyrdom. Thousands of Bábis were put to death in the cruellest ways imaginable (as the Bahá'ís are to this day in Iran).

> By the testimony of Bahá'u'lláh, that heroic youth [Quddús] . . . was subjected to such tortures and suffered such a death as even Jesus had not faced in the hour of His greatest agony. The absence of any restraint on the part of the government authorities, the ingenious barbarity which the torture-mongers of Bárfurúsh so ably displayed, and fierce fanaticism which glowed in the breasts of its shí'ah inhabitants, the moral support accorded to them by the dignitaries of Church and State in the capital — above all, the acts of heroism which their victim and his companions had accomplished and which had served to heighten their exasperation, all combined to nerve the hand of the assailants and to add to the diabolical ferocity which characterized his martyrdom. [49]

Táhirih, also, was put to death for her blasphemy. Adorned in "a gown of snow-white silk," [50] she met her executioners. Handing them a silken kerchief, the symbol of her purity since the days of her infancy, Táhirih underlined the meaning of her martyrdom. To her being strangled by this symbolic kerchief while wearing her wedding dress *was* her nuptial union with the new creation her actions had helped to release from the misogyny of Islam.

There is much to admire about Táhirih. In the symbolic action of her unveiling herself at Badasht, as in her martyr's death in Tihrán, we sense that the trauma that her religious tradition had so long propitiated had at least partially been absorbed into a new form. That she was both a woman and a poet is also suggestive here. However, when "meet[ing] [the] Beloved" [51] has the form of martyrdom, as it had in her case, that meeting has been in the spirit, not in the soul. The trauma released at Badasht was absorbed into a new religion, not into the simple soul-making of men and women.

Of course, there is an immense difference in scale between a religion-making martyr like Táhirih and the simple soul-making of the modern individual. This difference, however, is just the point. In our time, the spirit's traumatic intensity needs to be radically interiorized, reflected through our inhibitions, wrestled with as *the* neurosis and *our* neurosis at one and the same time. For meaning in the vast sense of religion requires too much blood. The world can no longer afford such devotion to its gods.

How man conceives of what might be called his metaphysical status is an immensely important problem. Jung's contribution to its clarification was to define the individual as "an immensely weighty milligram without which God had made his world in vain." [52] Making the same point in another way, Jung referred to psychology as "a sphere but lately visited by the numen, where the whole weight of mankind's problems has settled." [53] Against the macrocosmic background that martyrdom and religious terrorism provide, we may better appreciate what Jung was trying to do in making these assertions. While at first glance, these lines seem to inflate the significance of the individual and of psychotherapy, their actual intent may have been to scale back and reduce the absolute significance of the Trauma-God. Where religious man would devoutly identify with the trauma, putting the demands of its spirit before his own life, there is another task — the building of the earthly tabernacle through a devotion to the small-scale, the individual, the daily, and the unique. In a letter to a correspondent, Jung wrote:

> God wants to be born in the flame of man's consciousness, leaping ever higher. And what if this has no roots in the earth? If it is not a house of stone where the fire of God can dwell, but a wretched straw hut that flares up and vanishes? Could God then be born? One must be able to suffer God. That is the supreme task for the carrier of ideas. He must be the advocate of the earth. God will take care of Himself. [54]

Ministering to our trauma-ridden times, Jung emphasizes that it is the flame of man's consciousness, not the flames of a suicide bomber immolating himself or the flames of an embassy bombing, that God requires of man. It is now more important than ever to get this right.

Another quote from Jung is apt in the present context. It is a passage from a letter in which he discusses the same motif of which our account of Táhirih's martyrdom is an instance.

> The macrocosmic relationship presents a great difficulty. It shows itself symptomatically first in the form of an urge to make the microcosmic relationship objective, external, tangible. The *coniunctio* of the masculine and feminine halves of the self is apt to overpower the individual and force him into physical, i.e., cosmic, manifestation . . . [E]very archetype, before it is integrated *consciously*, wants to manifest itself physically, since it forces the subject into its own form. The self in its divinity (i.e., the archetype) is unconscious of itself. [55]

In these lines, Jung could be describing the religion-making martyr. In the rest of the passage, he emphasizes the importance of containing this manic tendency even as I spoke above about the simple soul-making of men and women.

> [The archetype] can *become conscious only within our consciousness.* And it can do that only if the ego stands firm. The self must become as small as, and yet smaller than, the ego although it is the ocean of divinity: "God is as small as me," says Angelus Silesius . . . The *hierosgamos* takes place in the vessel. In principle you are not the goddess, I am not the god, otherwise man would cease to be and God would not have been born. We can only stretch out our hands to each other and know the inner man. Superhuman possibilities are not for us. [56]

Turning the Tables

Heir to the enormous BANG with which the universe began, soul made its first appearance as the Gods through whom it responded to the obdurate conditions of its traumatic surround. Perhaps best described as the 'within of things,' soul came into the picture by pre-emptively turning Being's violent fullness against itself in the form of a whole plethora of images. It was these images, each at least minimally different from the outwardness of the things which they lit up from within, that bought wiggle-room, freedom, life, and will for the soul. How else but by turning the tables upon the determinate forces of the universe could the reflectedness of the psyche, the reflectedness of the soul, have brought itself forth?

Writing with reference to patterns in the soul that he variously called "primordial images," "archaic remnants," and most famously "archetypes," Jung makes a similar point about the soul's traumatic origins. Archetypes, he writes,

> . . . are the precipitate of the psychic functioning of the whole ancestral line; the accumulated experiences of organic life in general, a million times repeated, and condensed into types. In these . . . all experiences are represented which have happened on this planet since primeval times. The more frequent and the more intense they were, the more clearly focused they become in the archetype. [57]

What Jung here refers to as the "accumulated experiences of organic life . . . , a million times repeated," we may take as a reference to the traumatic exigencies of nature that have repeatedly inscribed themselves as memory, remembered themselves as soul. Interestingly, this connection is etymologically given with the word "archetype" itself. As Jung has noted, taken together the Greek roots *archē* (= origin) and *tupos* (= blow or imprint) present the notion of an originating imprint, a first blow. [58] Like the Gods who drew their sustenance from the killing blow of the sacrificer's axe, archetypes also have their source in trauma. [59]

Further to these references to Jung's work, a number of others beg to be cited here. I think, for example, of "Mind and Earth," an essay that treats of the mind as "a *system of adaptation determined by the conditions of an earthly environment.*" [60] In this essay the great psychologist looks back to "that prehistoric time when reindeer hunters fought for a bare and wretched existence against the elemental forces of wild nature." [61] Surely this is a reference to the traumas that have been the sources of our most primordial soul-making. And, then, in the seminar on dream analysis we find the following:

... a medicine-man has to go through hellish tortures. Eskimos hang them up by their toes or immerse them in icy water till they are nearly mad. Such a series of shocks pierces holes through which the collective unconscious comes in from all sides. Now, provided a man can stand the onslaught of things coming from below, he can influence other people, he can have an almost hypnotic effect on his fellow tribesmen. [62]

But what about that turning of the tables we mentioned above? How does this figure in Jung's thought about archetypes? Further to our just cited reference to the vision-quickening torments of the shaman, any of a number of passages could be quoted here. We shall content ourselves with a single one of these, from "The Psychology of the Child Archetype."

It is not the world as we know it that speaks out of [archaic man's] unconscious, but the unknown world of the psyche, of which we know that it mirrors our empirical world only in part, and that, for the other part, it moulds this empirical world in accordance with its own psychic assumptions. The archetype does not proceed from physical facts, but describes how the psyche experiences the physical fact, and in so doing the psyche often behaves so autocratically that it denies the tangible reality or makes statements that fly in the face of it. [63]

This account of the table-turning action of the archetypal psyche needs to be immediately qualified. While we may readily concur with Jung's point about the autocratic power of the psyche, we must also bear in mind that this "relative autonomy" (as it is sometimes also called) is only painfully acquired over a very long period.

A passage from Nietzsche speaks to this. Introducing his analysis of the constitution of man's conscience and memory, the traumatic philosopher asks, "How can one create a memory for the human animal? How can one impress something upon this partly obtuse, party flighty mind, attuned only to the passing moment, in such a way that it will stay there?" In line with our thesis concerning trauma, Nietzsche answers:

One can well believe that the answers and methods for solving this primeval problem were not precisely gentle;

perhaps indeed there was nothing more fearful and uncanny in the whole prehistory of man than his *mnemotechnics*. "If
something is to stay in the memory it must be burned in:
only that which never ceases to *hurt* stays in the memory"
— this is a main clause of the oldest (unhappily also the
most enduring) psychology on earth. One might even say
that wherever on earth solemnity, seriousness, mystery,
and gloomy coloring still distinguish the life of man and a
people, something of the terror that formerly attended all
promises, pledges, and vows on earth is *still effective*: the past,
the longest, deepest and sternest past, breaths upon us and
rises up in us whenever we become "serious." Man could
never do without blood, torture, and sacrifices when he felt
the need to create a memory for himself; the most dreadful sacrifices and pledges (sacrifices of the first-born among
them), the most repulsive mutilations (castration, for example), the cruellest rights of all the religious cults (and all
religions are at the deepest level systems of cruelties) — all
this has its origin in the instinct that realized that pain is
the most powerful aid to mnemonics. [64]

Nietzsche's mnemotechnics of religious cruelty, along with Jung's account the soul's having inscribed the exigencies of nature into itself in the
form of archetypes, lead us now to Wolfgang Giegerich's account of ritual
slaughtering as primordial soul-making. According to Giegerich, the history of consciousness, subjectivity, inwardness, and soul is a history of killings. Turning the tables on the obdurate conditions of life, soul killed itself
into existence, the form of this process being that of ritual sacrifice.

The dullness of animal existence had consisted in the fact that
the reaction to whatever was encountered had to be more of less
automatic (affective, instinctual), exclusively in the service of the
biological purpose of securing and heightening life. *Homo necans*
— the killing man — burst asunder this being bonded by naked
biological interests through his blow with the axe or thrusting the
spear. For with this tremendous deed he logically broke through
life's boundary to death, by which boundary the living organism
is completely enclosed; he thus inflicted the experience of death
upon himself, *while* still in life, and made this experience the basis
of his own, no longer merely-biological life. [65]

A Jungian analyst, Giegerich brings his argument to bear upon the notion of the archetype. With our focus on trauma in mind, let us hear him a little further on this subject:

> All Gods need sacrifices. Why? Because they have their existence, their reality, only in the sacrificial blow and blood. Our idea is that God or Gods are existing entities (if we accept the notion of God at all). But in ancient times Gods were nothing else but *the trembling of the soul* vis-à-vis the blow with the axe, a trembling which like the vibration of a musical string fades out in time and is therefore in need of renewal . . .
>
> In the sacrificial blow the soul drove the God images or archetypes into itself. Each killing blow imprinted the specific archetypal image in the soul afresh. [66]

If there is a contemporary resonance to Giegerich's account of the soul-constituting importance that ritual slaughtering had held for archaic man it is the resonance of an old habit dying hard. Though clearly killing and ritual sacrifice are no longer viable ways of soul-making in our time, they are still used by the members of dying faiths and backward nations as a means to set the soul trembling again. But power politics has long replaced religious awe, even for those nations which pretend that they have not divided Church from State. Despite their most concerted efforts, the martyr, the terrorist, and the suicide-bomber of today cannot really achieve the ends that they so deludedly seek by spilling new blood for such an old ceremony. The slaughter we watch nightly on the news is hardly awe-inspiring to anyone today. (The glee of a terrorist or of a nation manifesting its destiny is hardly awe.) Even an event as enormous as the collapse of the Twin Towers is paltry compared to media's capacity to render it into digitalized images. Effeteness and irreality are our trauma today, and no amount of blood seems able to move us from our dullness now.

1. In John (15:1–2, 4–6) the meaning of suffering as punitive correction persists:

> I am the true vine, and My Father is the vine-dresser. Every branch in Me that does not bear fruit, He takes away; and every branch that bears fruit, He prunes it, that it may bear more fruit … Abide in Me, and I in you. As the branch cannot bear fruit of itself, unless it abides in the vine, so neither can you, unless you abide in Me. I am the vine, you are the branches; he who abides in Me, and I in him, he bears much fruit; for apart from Me you can do nothing. If anyone does not abide in Me, he is thrown away as a branch and dries up; and they gather them, and cast them into the fire, and they are burned.

2. Hans Küng, *On Being a Christian* (New York: Doubleday, 1984), p. 435.

3. Ibid., p. 434.

4. Ludwig Feuerbach, *Das Wesen des Christenthums* (Leipzig: Otto Wigand, 1883), p. 111.

5. Cited by Reidar Thomte in *Kierkegaard's Philosophy of Religion* (New York: Greenwood Press, 1969), p. 83.

6. Søren Kierkegaard, *Concluding Unscientific Postscript to the "Philosophical Fragments,"* trans. David F. Swenson, ed. Walter Lowrie (Princeton: Princeton University Press & American-Scandinavian Foundation, 1941), p. 432.

7. Cited by Walter Kaufmann in *Nietzsche: Philosopher, Psychologist, Antichrist* (New York, Vintage Books, 1968), p. 356.

8 . James Hillman, *Re-Visioning Psychology*, p. 97.

9. Ibid., p. 95.

10. James Hillman, *Inter Views* (New York: Harper & Row, 1983), p. 76.

11. Ibid., p. 75.

12. A sentence by Jesus' from the Gospel of John (15:6) combines these two ideas and gives support to the view that the wrath of the Old Testament Father exists, as well, in the New Testament Son:

> If anyone does not abide in Me, he is thrown away [by God, the gardener] as a branch, and dries up; and they gather them, and cast them into the fire, and they are burned.

13. It may be objected at this point that God cannot be held responsible for the actions of those who act misguidedly in His name. Hillman has suggested, however, that every model structures its own uses and abuses and is thus responsible for both. It is not enough to say in hindsight that so and so

was a bad Christian. God and Jesus, being the original models upon which the behavior of the "bad believer" has been patterned, must not be exonerated from criticism. For Hillman's views about models and their shadows see Louis Zinkin, "Is There Still a Place For the Medical Model," in *Spring 1984* (Dallas: Spring Publications, 1984), p. 120.

14. Sigmund Freud and Joseph Breuer, "On the Theory of Hysterical Attacks," *CP* 5: 30.

15. C.S. Lewis, *The Problem of Pain* (New York: HaperCollins, 2001), p. 4.

16. Ibid.

17. Ibid.

18. Ibid., p. 78.

19. Ibid.

20. Ibid.

21. C.G. Jung, *CW* 16: 257.

22. Freud, *New Introductory Lectures on Psycho-Analysis* (Lecture 31), trans. W.J.H. Sprott (London: Hogarth, 1933), p. 78.

23. James Hillman, *Re-Visioning Psychology*, pp. 55-112.

24. Cited in Randolph Severson, "Puer's Wounded Wing: Reflections on the Psychology of Skin Disease." In J. Hillman, ed., *Puer Papers* (Irving, TX: Spring Publications, 1979), p. 132.

25. Ronald Fairbairn, "The Repression and the Return of the Bad Objects (with special reference to the 'war neuroses'). In *Psychoanalytic Studies of the Personality* (London: Tavistock, 1952), pp. 66–67.

26. C.S. Lewis, *The Problem of Pain*, p. 83.

27. Ibid.

28. Ibid., pp. 83–84.

29. Ibid., p. 85.

30. Cited by Lyn Cowan in *Masochism: A Jungian View* (Dallas: Spring Publications, 1982), p. 21.

31. Cited in ibid., p. 98.

32. St. Theresa of Avila carefully distinguished the wish-fulfilling aspect of the imagination from a true vision of God: "It happens to some people . . . that they become absorbed in their imagination to the extent that everything they think about seems to be clearly seen. Yet, if they were to see a real vision, they would know without any doubt whatsoever their mistake, for they themselves are composing what they see with their imagination." True vision, St. Theresa goes on to say, is entirely different from the wilful productions of the imagination: "In . . . vision . . . the soul is very far from thinking that anything will be seen, or having the thought even pass through its mind, suddenly the vision is represented to it all at once and stirs all the faculties and senses with a great fear and tumult so as to place them

afterward in that happy peace." *The Interior Castle*, trans. Kieran Kavanaugh and Otilio Rodriguez (New York: Paulist Press, 1979), p. 158.

33. St. Theresa of Avila, *The Life of Saint Theresa of Avila by Herself*, trans. J. M. Cohen (London, Penguin Books, 1957), p. 210.

34. Evelyn Underhill, *Mysticism: A Study in the Nature and Development of Man's Spiritual Development* (New York: E.P. Dutton & Co., 1961), p. 19.

35. P.B. Shelley, *Prometheus Unbound*, IV, lines 573–74.

36. A sentence of St. Paul's provides a scriptural basis for this behavior: "Therefore, since Christ has suffered in the flesh, arm yourselves also with the same purpose, because he who has suffered in the flesh has ceased from sin . . ." (I Peter 4:1)

37. Cited by Evelyn Underhill in *Mysticism: A Study in the Nature and Development of Man's Spiritual Consciousness*, p. 218.

37. Rudolf Otto, *The Idea of the Holy*, trans. John W. Harvey (London: Oxford University Press, 1958), pp. 191–92.

39. Anonymous.

40. Friedrich Nietzsche, *The Portable Nietzsche*, ed. and trans. Walter Kaufmann (New York: The Viking Press, 1968), p. 197.

41. P.B. Shelley, *Prometheus Unbound*, III, lines 201–03.

42. Ibid., lines 197–204.

43. Friedrich Nietzsche, *Joyful Wisdom*, trans. Thomas Common (New York: Frederick Ungar Publishing, 1960, p. 168.

44. R.D. Laing, *The Divided Self* (New York: Pantheon Books, 1969), p. 94.

45. Ibid., p. 95.

46. C.G. Jung, CW 9.1: 195.

47. Nabíl, *The Dawn-Breakers: Nabíl's Narrative Of The Early Days of the Bahá'í Revelation*, trans. Shoghi Effendi (Wilmette: Bahá'í Publishing Trust, 1970), p. 293.

48. Ibid., pp. 294–96.

49. Ibid., pp. 410–11.

50. Ibid, p. 622.

51. Ibid.

52. C.G. Jung, *Letters Vol. 1, 1906–1950*, ed. G. Adler (Princeton, N.J.: Princeton University Press, 1973), p. 338.

53. C.G. Jung, CW 16: 449.

54. C.G. Jung, *Letters Vol. 1, 1906–1950*, p. 65.

55. Ibid., p. 336.

56. Ibid.

57. C.G. Jung CW 6: 659.

58. C.G. Jung, CW 18: 523f.

59. Cf. Wolfgang Giegerich, "Killings: Psychology's Platonism and the Missing Link to Reality," in *Spring 54*: 5–18.

60. C.G. Jung, CW 10: 49.

61. C.G. Jung, CW 10: 55.

62. C.G. Jung, *Dream Analysis: Notes of the Seminar Given in 1928–1930*, ed. W. McGuire (Princeton: Princeton University Press, 1984), p. 328.

63. C.G. Jung, CW 9.1: 260.

64. Friedrich Nietzsche, *On the Genealogy of Morals* & *Ecce Homo*, trans. W. Kaufmann and R.J. Hollingdale (New York: Random House, 1969), pp. 60–61.

65. Wolfgang Giegerich, "Killings," p. 12.

66. Ibid., pp. 12–13.

chapter two


HEALING THROUGH HERESY

## The Infectious Savior

After her suicide attempt, shortly before her release from the psychiatric hospital, she dreamed that she sat in a bathtub with light shining out of her nostrils. She found that she was able to take the batteries out of her head, disconnecting the light. The scene changed. Back in her apartment, sitting at the typewriter, she watched workmen replace the glass window panes with white writing paper.

She told her friend the dream. He thought the dream psychotic. He thought that her ability to say the right things to the doctors to gain discharge reflected less her sanity than her deftness at taking batteries out of her flashlight head. He told her that he believed the dream was suggesting that writing could provide a container for what her life could not contain.

Later that evening while reading Northrop Frye's book, *The Great Code: The Bible and Literature*, he came upon a passage that brought the dream she had told him back to mind. Writing about Leviathan, the great chaos monster of the oceans, Frye quotes a description of the creature from Job 41:18: ". . . by his sneezings a light doth shine, and his eyelids are like the eyelids of the morning." Setting down the book, he pondered the connection between Leviathan and his friend's dream. "She *is* Leviathan," he thought. "Her psychosis is her identification with him. But how? How is it that this modern woman in a bathtub with batteries in her head manifests the chaos monster?"

He retired to bed, still preoccupied with this question. While sleeping he dreamed. He was on the front lawn of his parents' home. Before him on the grass lay a bathtub that was completely covered with crosses, Christian crosses. The crosses were drawn on the bathtub so densely that they formed together a cross-hatch or grid design. "Like graph-paper," he thought. Then he had a telephone in his hand. A man from England was on the line. The man said, "The anti-incarnational ideas you are now conceiving are very, very, evil." The scene changed, amplifying the dream in other images. He was working on a fishing trawler. Huge catches of fish (fish = Christ) were being heaved on board in nets. The mesh of the nets

reminded him of the crosses (or was this but an afterthought upon waking
and recalling the dream?). Looking down at his legs, he was fascinated to
notice that his blue jeans were entirely patterned with a cross-hatch design
of densely arranged crosses. Again the scene changed. He watched an artist
make a grid of lines on a drawing. The grid of lines broke the picture into
small units. The artist could then transpose the drawing to a larger grid or
a smaller one, scaling the picture up or scaling it down.

In the morning he awoke full of dreams, his friend's from the day before and his own from the night past. "Jesus," he thought, "is it through you
that the spirit enters flesh, that Leviathan enters bathtubs and persons?
Your cross scales the non-human, archetypal world down into man. Are
you the carrier and source of the contagion from which we suffer?"

Gnosticism

The Gnostic did not deny trauma. He denied that Christ suffered it for
us. In the *Acts of John*, a work of Christian Apocrypha cut from the biblical
canon on account of its evident Gnostic features, the gospel writer takes
us to a cave in the Mount of Olives shortly after Jesus was nailed to the
cross. In the cave John wept for his crucified Lord. But when a darkness
came over the whole earth, Christ appeared to John, filled the cave with
light and said,

> John, for the people below in Jerusalem I am being crucified
> and pierced with lances and reeds and given vinegar and gall to
> drink. But to you I am speaking, and listen to what I speak.

Having declared himself, the Christic phantom (it is ambiguous whether
he is corporeal or not) revealed to John the mystery of the cross of light:

> . . . he showed me a cross of light firmly fixed, and around the
> cross a great crowd, which had no single form; and in the cross
> was one form and the same likeness. And I saw the Lord him-
> self above the cross, having no shape but only a kind of voice;

yet not that voice which we knew, but one that was sweet and gentle and truly the voice of God, which said to me, "John, there must be one man to hear these things from me; for I need one who is ready to hear. This cross of light is sometimes called logos by me for your sakes, sometimes mind, sometimes Jesus, sometimes Christ, sometimes a door, sometimes a way, sometimes bread, sometimes seed, sometimes resurrection, sometimes Son, sometimes Father, sometimes Spirit, sometimes life, sometimes truth, sometimes faith, sometimes grace; and so it is called for men's sake. [1]

This revelation is not simply a defense — John's clinging to the lost object through what Freud would call "a hallucinatory wish-psychosis." [2] This gospel was written between the second and forth centuries A.D. and is not the literal story of John's experience on the Mount of Olives. If it were we would be tempted to see it as an example of denial pure and simple: unable to face the death of his Lord, John denies the crucifixion with a wishful, mystical vision. But this gospel is not reducible to John's security operations. It is not simply the denial of Christ's death and suffering. It is a Gnostic-Docetist rejection of vicarious atonement. The denial is not of death and suffering; denied is the theological conception that salvation has the single formulation of Christ crucified on a wooden cross (i.e., corporeally, once and for all, at a specific time and place in history).

One story is not enough in the Gnostic view. Christ, for the Gnostic, has many names and many faces. He appears to each soul in accordance with the capacity of each soul. In another text from the Apocryphal collection, the *Acts of Peter*, "Peter" witnesses the Transfiguration of Christ on Mount Tabor. The vision was actually a group vision. A whole crowd witnessed the transfiguration, each in their own way. *Talem eum vidi qualem capere potui*, Peter explains: "I saw him in such a form as I was able to take in." [3]

The intent of Gnosticism is to gain knowledge and renewal by pushing religious thought to the brink of heresy and beyond. By means of a new gospel every day, the Gnostic sought to penetrate out of the reified canon of approved gospels and into the process of *gospelizing*. Gnosticism, first and foremost, is a proliferation of books, an archeological find of fifty-two texts at Nag Hammadi, an embarrassment of riches.

In the place of the dogmatic truth of the wooden cross, Gnosticism places the subtle cross, the cross of light, metaphor. Gnosticism is based not in holy writ, but in the holiness of writing itself. It is not the story of Christ that brings salvation; it is the storying-Christ. The incorporeal (non-incarnate) Gnostic-Jesus is metaphor, and metaphor is the uncanonical solution for the Old Testament trauma, the Old Testament God. Gnosticism is healing fiction.

The nailing of Christ to the wooden cross was, in the Gnostic view, the crucifixion of the capacity to make fiction, the nailing of metaphor, literalism. On the Mount of Olives, Christ reveals this to be the true nature of his suffering:

> You hear that I suffered, yet I suffered not; and that I suffered not, yet I did suffer; and that I was pierced, yet I was not wounded; that I was hanged, yet I was not hanged; that blood flowed from me, yet it did not flow, and, in a word, that what they say of me, I did not endure, but what they do not say, those things I did suffer. Now what these are, I secretly show you . . . You must know me, then, as the torment of the logos, the piercing of the logos, the blood of the logos, the wounding of the logos, the fastening of the logos. [4]

## Gnostic Analysis

The analyst behind the couch is the gnostic on the Mount of Olives. The patient lying before him is the corporeal Jesus nailed to the wooden cross. With benign indifference, the analyst listens as the patient recounts the history of his incarnational life. Dreams and associations are analyzed to discover the complexes in which spirit is trapped. Ideally, the relationship between them is an optimally frustrating one (in Kohut's sense). For a too gratifying relationship would only further the incarnational pull that would bind the pair to what Shelley, in his *Defence of Poetry*, calls "the accidents of surrounding impressions." But the job of analysis, or at least of a gnostic analysis, is to liberate spirit from the contingency of the patient's life through metaphor. Should the analyst leave his station behind the couch, or should the patient be allowed access to the analyst on extra-analytical or personal terms, all metaphors would be instantly attenuated and the spirit would be trapped in matter once more.

St. Paul said that the first birth is of the earth, the second of heaven. Pulling this adage toward our present purposes (even as Jung had it carved upon his tombstone), we may say that a gnostically-conceived analysis does not aim to repeat the intercourse that has made for the patient's *first* birth. Rather, by means of a sublter union, its aim is to reveal the primal scene, interrupt the parental coitus, and free the soul from its Oedipal bondage.

The royal road of re-generation, discarnation, and metaphor is the enigmatic, identity-subverting relationship, which psychoanalysis calls transference. Essentially unknown, the analyst behind the couch is more than an idealized father or mother imago. Quietly present, he is the father and mother (or whatever else) of absence, the gate of the *deus absconditus*. The more the patient speaks to him, the more uncertain they both become. Gradually, the analytic discourse breaks up the patient's account of his incarnational life to the point where suddenly his words are no longer bound to it at all. The couch becomes a subtle couch, a couch of light, a Mount of Olives, a metaphor. Reclining in the repose of metaphor, the patient is released from the prose of his incarnational life. By restating in poetic terms the incidents of his life which the language of prose had preserved as trauma, the patient frees his soul to follow its desires.

Trauma in the Transference

"Religious ideas," writes Freud, "have arisen from the same need as have all the other achievements of civilization: from the necessity of defending oneself against the crushingly superior force of nature." [5] Reflecting further upon this assertion in the light of a main tenet of his analytic theory, Freud continues ". . . when man personifies the forces of nature he is . . . following an infantile model. He has learned from the persons in his earliest environment that the way to influence them is to establish a relation with them; and so, later on, with the same end in view, he treats everything else that he comes across in the same way as he treated those persons." [6]

Turning our usual concern about the traumas to which children are subject in family on its head, the Freud of these passages may be read as laying bear the psyche's tendency to propitiate overwhelming events in religio-familial terms. Though children, to be sure, frequently are traumatized in family by parents, and though this is a prolific source of the transferences that compel and inhibit future relationships, it is also the case that the familial *metaphor* is called into play as a basic mode of propitiating *any* overwhelming event whatsoever. Condensing this insight into an adage (the better to keep it constantly in mind), let us say *that whatever traumatizes us becomes our parent. Or, putting this another way, let us say that whatever we cannot master with our creating will, we turn into a super-parent or god and are infantilized by it.*

Heir to the archetype we have just described (Jung regarded "husband, wife, father, mother, child" to be "the mightiest archetypes of all . . ." [7]), patients in psychotherapy routinely project the imagos of the parents onto their therapists, or familialize their otherwise unrepresentable needs and traumas by transferentially representing them in such terms. Like the Psalmist invoking God's good side against His bad side, they try to cuddle up to the "crushingly superior forces" of their inner and outer worlds in the person of the parent-therapist. But no illusion, however comforting, can last forever. Even when there is a warm rapport between the patient and therapist, transference is ultimately a chilly cuddle, the boundaries of therapy being what they are. Sessions come abruptly to an end. Holidays feel like abandonments. The analyst's silence like rejection and judgement at times. Re-doubling the adaptive strategy described above by Freud, the patient regresses still further in search of the power he swayed as a baby over his familial environment. By hook or by crook, trumped up mishap or real trauma, the therapist will *be* the loving or hating parent, or so the patient unconsciously demands.

But lo, just here the lyric of an old blues number passes through the mind: "mama may have, and papa may have, but God bless the child that's got his own . . ." [8] In keeping with this line, a main task of psychotherapy is to bring to light the patient's lingering tendency to form covenantal relationships on the archetypal model of the family constellation so that the real challenge which outer forces and inner imperatives present can be taken up and the patient may come into his own. Having seen through his patients' masochistic regress-to-conquer mode of seeking gratification, safety, and control, Freud placed his chair behind the couch. In this way he anchored psychoanalysis at a point of empathy-tempering remove from the family romance that his supine patients were so often trying to seduce it into as transference. To have uncritically accepted the stories he heard — even when they were leaven with a good deal of truth — would have been to allow himself, in the transference, to be turned into an abuser-in-reverse, the good trauma carrier, the good parent. Recognizing this, Freud created a method that is conducive to the patients becoming conscious of their seductive, familializing tendency to projectively identify their wishes, needs, yearnings, and pain into others rather than grappling with these soulfully for themselves.

Today, more and more, psychotherapy seems to be falling in for the model of therapy that Freud eschewed. Many therapists today describe what they do as "re-parenting." Therapy as re-parenting can take any number of forms, from the nurturing ethos of a patriarchy-resenting feminist therapy to the concrete literalism of an Esalen re-birthing weekend. The problem with practices of this kind, however, is that the patient merely adopts a good parent to replace the bad; nothing is experienced, save the bogey-trumping transference resistances through which the unfamilar is warded off as trauma and the genuinely traumatic is hallowed and preserved. No wonder the so-called transference neurosis is so hard to resolve. More and more therapy hours must be sacrificed to mollify the demands of the familialized trauma — the fierce incest wishes of the transference. Of course analysis becomes an interminable endeavor. The love-cure, when acted out, is a very difficult thing to give up.

The acting-out that we have just critiqued has more subtle and sophisticated versions. In this connection, we may think of the familial lens which psychoanalysis shares in common with its patients. As personified agents of causality, the figures of the parents are huge etiological presences in the case histories of psychotherapy. Like its patients, who resort to the familial metaphor in the face of the unknown, psychology iatrogenically reinforces this tendency by its Oedipal and pre-Oedipal sense of what constitutes clinical material. Is this why the grief-bringing insight — that even if the therapist could be what the patient wants him to be it would not do him the good it would have done in the needful moment of the past — now takes a longer and longer analysis to achieve?

Keenly aware of the fact that even "Freud's theory of neurosis — so admirably suited to the nature of neurotics — [is] much too dependent on the neurotic ideas from which precisely the patients suffer," [9] Jung maintained that it is not just the patient that must demolish or abrogate the Oedipus complex in the unconscious, as Freud asserted, [10] but psychology, too. For ". . . the real therapy only begins when the patient sees that it is no longer father and mother who are standing in his way, but himself — i.e., an unconscious part of his personality which carries on the role of father and mother." Jung continues:

> Even this realization, helpful as it is, is still negative; it simply says, "I realize that it is not father and mother who are against me, but I myself." But *who* is it in him that is against him? What is this mysterious part of his personality that hides under the father- and mother-imagos, making him believe for years that the cause of his trouble must somehow have got into him from outside? This is the counterpart of his conscious attitude, and it will leave him no peace and will continue to plague him until it has been accepted. [11]

Rosemary's Baby

The collective unconscious, as the "deposit of thousands of years of experience of the struggle for existence and adaptation," [12] stands in a compensatory relationship to the traumas of our lives. Like some "2,000,000-year-old man" [13] who has absorbed a virtual infinity of traumas, it underpins the resilience of the self, bringing the healing balm of its knowing in the form of "mighty images." [14] Like some God ever-nigh, it hears the sparrow fall. But this is only the light half of the story. On a darker note, we must also recognize that the collective unconscious is not immune to the passage of time. The covenants it made with our ancestors gradually lose their efficiency and stand in need of renewal. Struggling once again for existence and adaptation, psyche must seek to renew its responses through our lives and our circumstances. As in the beginning of the Christian story, the problem once again becomes how to get a virgin pregnant. But even this old metaphor does not quite suffice any longer, the unprecedented rapidity of change having queered the pitch in the meantime.

At junctures such as those just described, where there is a failure of fit between the world and the manner in which our psychic structure anticipates that world, what Bion called the "mating" of mind and matter backfires into what Jung called "incest." When this occurs every event that impinges upon the self feels like incestuous abuse, those we love and depend on like the minions of the Trauma-God. Blaming our nurture for whatever has affronted our nature, we turn backwards upon our parents and circumstances, feeling raped by what they did or did not do to us. Alternatively, needing to preserve our sense of the goodness of our kin and kind, we may reject these home-spun versions of the seduction theory and visit our reproaches upon ourselves instead. It is not that we have been maltreated or misused; it is our own dark designs that are at the bottom of our troubles. Like Freud before us, though less heroically, we press on in our self-analysis, making each of the central discoveries of psychoanalysis on ourselves — infantile sexuality, the Oedipus complex, repetition compulsion and the death instinct. Attacking our innocence with Luciferian insights of this sort, we self-protectively prevent ourselves from venturing into the fray of life where we might be traumatized again. Meanwhile, something grows in the womb of our symptoms, a huge fibroid perhaps, or an ominous tumor. Our dreams show a deformed monster-child living in the cellar, or a bull-rush basket in the effluent of a factory drain, or a Martian in a manger . . . Of course, it is difficult to say what really happened. Cause and effect notwithstanding, as far as *experience* is concerned, reality is a subjective phenomenon. Unable, as Freud said, to "distinguish between truth and fiction that has been cathected with affect," [15] we feel as buggered by the father we never knew as by the pedophile we did know. For, inasmuch as the angel that we also are demands a union that we can never fully realize, the pain of its yearning will register itself in our dreams, fantasies, and the constructions of analysis as a sexual trauma. No wonder the religious instinct so readily expresses itself as pedophilia. No wonder that on the way to rebirth we are always complaining that it is Rosemary's baby.

God Passes By

Why is it that "the falcon can no longer hear the falconer"? Why is it that God no longer hears the sparrow fall? Is it because there is no falconer? Is it because there is no God? Are the dialectical materialists correct? Do our falcons fly off and our sparrows fall because we have failed each other as husbands and wives, parents and children? What is the archetypal (as opposed to the personalistic) dimension of the calamities that befall ordinary people?

When bad things happen to good people it is not, let me insist, simply because other people were bad to them, though this they may have been. The insufficiency or evil of others provides at most the efficient cause of the calamity which the innocent suffer. Likewise, when a child goes wrong it is not merely because of the errors of the parents, though these cannot be dismissed. A child and its family go wrong because the culture in which they are embedded has lost its connection to what Jung has called the childhood aspect of the collective psyche.

Unable to sight the star above the stable of our times (though there be UFOs and crop circles aplenty), we turn instead to the science of those sunken Magi, the experts, for their not-so-sage advice. But when the instrumental rearing of children becomes more important than the raising up of new cultural forms, surely the Decline of the West, which Spengler forecast, must be reckoned to have come to pass. No wonder that the first words uttered by children today are not "momma" or "papa" but "get a life."

Unable to see the creature from outer space that our children have hidden away in their closets, contemporary culture would have us time our kids out in a corner of that Skinner box that our homes and our schools have become until they can behave in a properly secular manner. Instead of mediating the archetype through our cultural forms, instead of being in our various roles the domestic form of this mediation, we disintegrate into titanically reactive versions of the coarseness we now feast our eyes upon on reality TV. Little wonder that the soul reacts so delinquently. How else but through heretical acts, delinquent pranks, and reforming violence (or the inhibited form of these, apathetic withdrawal and underachievement) can the religious instinct reassert itself in the little Calvins, Luthers, and John Wesleys of our day?

Clement of Alexandria said that to know oneself is to know God. The opposite, however, is also true: it is through knowledge of God(s) that we come to know ourselves. But it is precisely here where the trouble starts — and by trouble I mean the suicidal teenager, the skin-head gang, David Karesh of the Wacko Texas tragedy. These troubled souls precisely take the measure of that alienation we each simultaneously have from ourselves and God — and it is for precisely this reason that the likes of a Karesh could claim to speak for God.

Though it is currently fashionable to explain the calamity of an individual life against the background of that individual's family experiences and development, a compete account cannot ignore the culture's failure to adequately come to terms with the contents of the collective unconscious that have lost their mediation in our time. Individuation is not merely about separating out from attachment-figures, nor does it consist solely of an incarnation of the latent potentials of the self — for the soul itself, in a more collective or transpersonal sense, is constantly unfolding, constantly being revolutionized. Religious ideas such as the Adamic cycle and progressive revelation bore an intuitive witness to this perennially creationist aspect of the soul's life. And in sunken form, this witness continues if only on the backwards now in the delusions of the insane. It is because we have lost our intuition of the soul's unfolding and are living in dispensations that have been rendered redundant, if not extinct, by subsequent mutations of consciousness, that people succumb to madness. Godlessly out of step with the new articulation of the spirit, and, yet, forgetting the call to "imagine no religion," we ourselves become parodies of the Gods we no longer believe in. Little wonder that we are so often such a trauma to each other.

## Assault On Freud

When we read Masson's book, *The Assault on Truth: Freud's Suppression of the Seduction Theory*, we are taken down into Jerusalem to the scene of a cruci-fixion. Freud's letters to Fliess recounting the complications suffered by Emma Eckstein due to their treatment of her are nothing less than horrific. Equally appalling is the material in the chapter which reviews the early literature of child abuse. Reading Masson's account of the origins of psy-choanalysis, we are overwhelmed by the trauma — both in the etiology of the cases and, in the instance of Emma Eckstein, in the treatment.

How is it that Freud could recant his seduction theory when it was so clearly grounded in the empirical record? Was it simply out of a failure of courage and a loyalty to Fliess as Masson argues?

Psychoanalysts generally view Freud's rejection of the seduction theo-ry and his discovery of the pathogenic power of fantasy as the foundation of psychoanalysis. The move from seduction in the outer sense of sexual abuse at the hands of others to seduction in the inner sense of disturbances caused by one's own drive fantasies was the beginning of what we call mod-ern psychology.

Like the gospel writer of the *Acts of John*, Freud's thought moved from the wooden cross of Jerusalem to the subtle cross of the Mount of Olives; that is, it moved from the carnal intelligence of the traumatic happenings that neither Freud nor his patients were able to entirely credit or absorb to a subtle, metaphorical intelligence, an intelligence that was able to soul-fully reflect traumatic events in the mirror of fantasy.

Freud's "rejection" of the seduction theory (if that is what it was) stemmed from the fact that at that time he did not adequately distinguish between events and experiences. Freud evaluated the veracity of the trau-matic events his patients remembered in analysis as if these events were *experiences*. Since the events, considered from the inside (i.e., psychoanalyti-cally), did not meet the outer criterion of being an experience, Freud came to doubt the reality of the events themselves. As he wrote to Fliess, "there are no indications of reality in the unconscious, so that one cannot distinguish between truth and fiction that has been cathected with affect." [16] Freud came to doubt the material reality of the traumas his patients reported because, at that time, he did not yet have a sufficiently differentiated concept of psychological reality to bridge the difference between the external events and the fantasies about them, which were making them into soul. In hindsight, however, we can see Freud's move away from the material basis of his patient's memories as the extremity necessary at the time (but no longer necessary today) to break out of his nineteenth-century materialism and into reality of the psyche, where events are made into experiences.

A trauma, by definition, is overwhelming and, for the most part, outside the available parameters of experience. Repression, it follows, is less a defensive procedure than an awkward terminology for expressing that an event lacks the sufficient field of comparison to be experienced as a discreet, delimited phenomenon. A traumatic event is not pushed out of awareness; rather, it is too big to register in awareness. Traumata only return from repression when a sufficient inventory of comparable events provides a reality schema that can more or less absorb them. The so-called repetition compulsion is a way of trying to create the field of comparable events in whose terms the traumatic event can be relativized and experienced. Of course, in the transference some sexually abused patients manufacture fictitious seduction scenes and attempt to seduce their therapists even while feeling menaced by the prospect of being abused by them. They act out what they cannot remember because it was too overwhelming to be properly experienced. They are trying to heal themselves.

Simply exposing the heinous deeds of seduction — objectively, externally, forensically — is of little help therapeutically. Therapy's concern is with absorbing the events, experiencing them. To play the good parent and point out to the patient in love and compassion that they have suffered an intolerable trauma is to confine their experience and the integration of their trauma to a good-parent / bad-parent split in conformity with society's disgust and horror. This kind of therapeutic maneuver merely shifts the trauma from matter to spirit. The patient identifies with his good parent or savior therapist and hovers now as far above the trauma as he once cowered beneath it. 'Born again,' a crusader for the oppressed or for this or that moral issue, the patient has merely identified with the whitewashed and reified version of what he could not absorb. Therapy has become vicarious religion and, inasmuch as the patient forfeited to it the drive to experience the events he has suffered (i.e., his compulsion to repeat), he has lost his soul.

Today, as heirs to Freud's psychological legacy, we can help our abused patients transmute their traumas into experiences. We can affirm the reality of child sexual assault and the mental disturbances that may accompany it precisely because we have been a hundred years on the Mount of Olives with Freud.

Freud's rejection of the seduction theory was not an "assault on truth," as Jeffrey Masson argues. It was the discovery of the metaphorical basis of the mind necessary to ground life's material (and spiritual) traumas in a fashion that heals them.

"You hear that I suffered, yet I suffered not; and that I suffered not, yet I did suffer . . ." Psychoanalysis eschews the crucifixion of the logos, the subordination of metaphorical language to the forensic reportage of "what happened." Psychoanalysis is a "talking cure," a re-writing of paralyzing events into experiences that let life go on.

Globus Hystericus

At the age of twelve, he experienced a severe trauma. A piece of food became lodged over his windpipe, choking him. The episode lasted a dangerously long time. So long, in fact, that the boy's soul slipped free from his body and ascended to the kitchen ceiling. From this vantage-point (we may think again of the gnostic on the Mount of Olives), he was able to dispassionately observe the commotion below — his mother's frantic efforts, his siblings' terrified looks, the top of his father's head. Finally, his mother was able to dislodge the obstruction. The blue-skinned boy could breath again. From behind a newspaper, the boy's father, sternly tightened up against his own fear, was yelling at his wife not to hit their son so hard on the back. After catching his breath, the boy yelled back: "What would you have her do — not save my life?"

The boy was never the same after that. The three-or four-minute so-
journ to the kitchen ceiling aged him. Already at twelve, he became an old
man — an old man and a philosopher, too. Not a philosopher of life, so
much, as a philosopher of his symptoms. Chief among these was his enormous difficulty swallowing, particularly when he ate with his father. For
many years he suffered as a result of this.

From the family systems perspective of Murray Bowen, this boy was
the "projected child," the child designated by the family to absorb its emotional fusion, the child through whom the marital conflict was short-cir-
cuiting. From a psychoanalytic point of view, trauma at the phallic stage of
development (perhaps adding itself to earlier oral conflicts returning from
repression with the re-constellation of the Oedipus complex at puberty)
had interrupted the normal resolution of the Oedipus complex. While
normally a son will have aligned himself with his father by this time in
order not to have him as an adversary, this boy perceived his father as too
ill-disposed toward him for identification to occur. From yet a third point
of view, the point of view of vicarious religion, Christ had died on the cross
that this boy might have life more abundant. If he could only take Jesus
into his life, Jesus would heal him by suffering it for him.

The boy was interested in this third possibility. He had been raised in
the church; he knew the Christian story. At some level he even felt close to
Jesus. Both were, after all, passover lambs — Jesus taking on the sins and
sufferings of the world, the choking boy the emotional fusion of his family system. Surely Christianity could resolve the boy's Oedipus complex.
Christ also had a murdering father and yet was able to commend his spirit
into his father's hands while being crucified by His design. Vicarious religion, however, did not heal the boy — though not for a lack of prayer and
supplication, both personal and intercessory.

When he was sixteen he had a dream. In the dream, he was back at the
friend's house he had been in the evening before. They were having the
same conversation about world religions. The evening before the dream,
the friend (a recent initiate to transcendental meditation) had explained
that there are 3 million gods in the Hindu pantheon, though all can be
considered aspects of the one deity, Brahman. In the dream, the party of
friends decide to move their conversation from the kitchen/family room
into the living room so as not to disturb the young host's parents who were

sleeping in a room nearby. As he was walking out of the room and into the hallway leading to the living room, the dreamer noticed an arching doorway and beyond that a small stone chapel. At the front of the little chapel a cross was erected in the chancel. The peculiar thing about the cross was that it was dismantled; the crosspiece to which the hands of Christ were nailed was lying down on the floor. The cross was beautiful and it emitted a holy light that illuminated the whole room.

Of course, the dreamer did not understand the dream intellectually. He had never heard of the Gnostics, let alone of the Docetist theology of the cross of light. Yet he did experience their revelation. The Hindu idea that God has 3 million faces must have triggered the dream. The idea is comparable to the notion presented in the *Acts of Peter* that each soul perceives God (Jesus) in such a form as it is able to take in. After this dream the boy's relation to his symptom lost its orthodoxy and changed. The cross, having been dismantled, could no longer serve as a model for his suffering or as a model for his vicarious salvation from suffering. If there were at least 3 million stories through which to experience God (i.e., the trauma he had learned to call God), what was his particular story?

While down in Jerusalem Christ was being nailed to a wooden cross and a twelve-year-old boy was gagging on his Oedipus complex, up on the Mount of Olives the same boy (though now sixteen) was realizing in a dream that the secret nature of his suffering was the crucifixion of the imagination by a single, reified, authorized version of the soul's atonement, the literalization of the logos.

The boy had literary ambitions. He wanted to be a writer. But how had the writing been going on for the past four years? It had been going on elaborately in a thousand little avoidance behaviors a day. The calligraphy in which he wrote his life had been a subversive calligraphy of hiding his symptoms and propitiating his trauma. For years he had lived a very circumscribed life, avoiding social engagements that would involve food. He had become the scribe of his trauma, utterly subservient to the dictates of the creative power he had renounced and projected into the unpalatable eucharist of vicarious religion.

The capacity within himself to absorb his own trauma, the capacity within himself to create his own sustaining fiction, had been rendered outcast, subversive, illegitimate and ineffectual by the story of Christ crucified. What he had been unable to swallow was the eucharist of vicarious theology.

After the dream of the dismantled cross, the boy's attention turned away from his symptom somewhat. More and more energy began to flow into writing. He wrote a black-humored novel about his symptom, comparable in some respects to Kafka's *Metamorphosis*. Sentence by sentence he transfigured into art the creative energy that had been incarnated into a neurotic lifestyle. Finally, enough writing had been done to render the body of his affliction into the *simulacrum* of a body. His symptoms had become a fiction. The *globus hystericus* had been cured by the wafer of soul-making metaphor.

## Do-It-Yourself

In the dream, he carefully drew a serpentine line on a piece of paper, a line that snaked back and forth like a serpent. A friend looked at the line with him, and together they adjusted it, making it even more serpentine. The scene changed. The dreamer found himself in a small-town Protestant church. The sanctuary was bright and lovely and full of the activity of a lively, singing congregation. It was also very plain. He didn't notice any stained glass or religious objects. Although the congregation was entirely Caucasian, they reminded him of a congregation of black gospel singers, so soulful was their music. He was enjoying the service immensely.

A cousin of his, a woman whom he had not seen since he was a child, sang a beautiful solo. Although she was the dreamer's cousin, her appearance was quite different. She had marked Jewish features (the dreamer was from a thoroughly Christian background) and was obviously mentally retarded. This mental deficiency did not detract at all from her singing; in fact, her moronic face smiled as if it were completely congruent with the pleasure of her song. Then the dreamer walked up to the table in the chancel. Although the communion table is the place of Christianity's central sacrament, this one was very plain. As communion tables go, it too was a smiling moron. On the table was a muffin, homemade, wholesome, and decorated with variously colored icing. He picked it up and tasted it.

The pleasant taste of the muffin was consistent with the pleasure and gaiety of the whole service — the warmth of community, the beauty of his cousin's voice and face, the songs themselves.

There are, of course, many ways to read this dream. One obvious way would be to see it as a demonic parody of Christianity — to see the snake as evil, the muffin as blasphemed eucharist, the dream itself as the sin against the Holy Ghost. Such an interpretation, however, is grounded in an orthodoxy that is foreign to the dream. Rather than measuring the dream's images against the reified sacramental standards they seem to be standing in for, let us stay closer to the images as they are, unconverted, un-amplified. This is not to deny that in this specific dream the conventional theological and sacramental forms are very present in their absence. The religious forms, which the dream's images seem to be standing in for, are indeed precisions of the dream's actual images. An essential aspect of the dream-church is that it lacks the sanctimonious quality we usually associate with a church. Everything about the dream-church is mundane; nothing is numinous. The architectural structure of the building expresses no heavenly striving. No heavenly scenes ornament the windows in stained glass. No cross is displayed as a focus of worship. *Nothing whatsoever in this church is vicarious.* The eucharist is a homemade muffin; the music is homespun soul; the service is an informal service without a presiding clergyperson. Even the soloist is a relative, a cousin of the dreamer.

In this do-it-yourself church there is no sense of displaced, reified suffering and vicarious atonement. The reach of the spirit has not exceeded the grasp of soul-making. A conjectured God does not reach beyond the parishioners' creating wills. There is no excess of God to be killed by some Nietzschean madman.

In his poem, "Esthétique du mal," Wallace Stevens takes up the same theme as does this dream. In explanation of his observation that "heaven and hell / Are one, and here, O terra infidel," Stevens writes:

> The fault lies with an over-human god,
> Who by sympathy has made himself a man
> And is not to be distinguished, when we cry

Because we suffer, our oldest parent, peer
Of the populace of the heart, the reddest lord,
Who has gone before us in experience.

If only he would not pity us so much,
Weaken our fate, relieve us of woe both great
And small, a constant fellow of destiny,

A too, too human god, self-pity's kin
And uncourageous genesis . . . It seems
As if the health of the world might be enough.

It seems as if the honey of common summer
Might be enough, as if the golden combs
Were part of a sustenance itself enough,

As if hell, so modified, had disappeared,
As if pain, no longer satanic mimicry,
Could be borne, as if we were sure to find our way. [17]

If it were not for the "too human god" of vicarious theology, the "honey of common summer" — the pleasures of the imagination, the muffin, and the song — would be enough to carve out a human habitation within the traumatic level of existence. In the dream and in Stevens's poem, vicarious religion is rejected in favor of the pleasure principle — soul-making, aesthetics, poetry, art. This is the serpent's wisdom, the serpentine, Gnostic line. Trauma, in the view of Gnostic-Docetism, cannot be packed off once and for all onto the shoulders of Christ crucified. Nor can a limited canon of approved gospels absorb "chance and death, and mutability." The meaning of a gospel is another gospel. Trauma involves us in an endless, serpentine process and the creative efforts of the imagination reflect the interminable dialectic between the reality and pleasure principles.

The imagination is like the song of our moronic, Jewish cousin. Her blank mind is the erasure of the Old Testament history of covenants with that upwardly displaced trauma we have learned to call God. Had Moses heard this cousin's singing, he might never have needed to bring the tablets down from Sinai. Had the Children of Israel heard this cousin's singing, they might never have needed to *worship* the calf they had made. For, from

the perspective of her song, both engagements are vicarious conjectur-
ings, conceits of belief rather than creations of the imagination for the
soul's delight.

### Romanticism

He went to a lecture at the University on the poetry of the English
Romantics. The lecturer suggested that the theme of Romanticism, whatever its content, was the process of its own making. The poets, he said,
were writing about writing. They were trying to build a temple for the soul
"Where branched thoughts, new grown with pleasant pain, / Instead of
pines shall murmur in the wind." The lecturer quoted a passage from John
Keats's famous letter:

> Call the world if you Please "The vale of Soul-making" Then
> you will find out the use of the world (I am speaking now in the
> highest terms for human nature admitting it to be immortal
> which I will here take for granted for the purpose of showing a
> thought which has struck me concerning it) I say "*Soul-making*"
> Soul as distinguished from an Intelligence — There may be
> intelligences or sparks of divinity in millions — but they are
> not Souls till they acquire identities, till each one is personally
> itself. I[n]telligences are atoms of perception — they know and
> they see and they are pure, in short, they are God — How then
> are Souls made? How then are these sparks which are God to
> have identity given them — so as ever to possess a bliss peculiar
> to each one's individual existence? How, but by the medium
> of a world like this? This point I sincerely wish to consider
> because I think it a grander system of salvation than the chrys-
> tean religion . . . [18]

Later that night, at home in bed, he drifted off into the culture, he
drifted off into a dream. On the lawn beside St. Paul's Anglican Church,
a tent was pitched and tightly zipped up. In the grass around the tent
lay money — loose coins, change. He was with friends. He and they were
local boys. They were maverick, delinquent, and uproarious. The scene

changed. He was listening to the repetition of last evening's lecture on the Romantics. While the lecturer spoke, he held the dreamer's head tightly between his hands. This show of affection was slightly embarrassing to the dream-ego. At last, the lecturer released his hold and the dreamer swooned. The hands had been holding the dreamer's head very tightly, cutting off the blood. The dreamer struggled to remain conscious and did manage to keep his wits. Then he noticed an article written by the lecturer titled, "Elegy." With the article was a polemic by a literary critic condemning the piece as mad or evil. Female custodians, fascinated with the lecture, allowed the talk to go on past the university's usual closing time. Finally, the lecture ended and the lecturer invited a dark woman to join him and they left together.

Then the time orientation shifted back to the middle of the lecture. The dreamer left the lecture hall, perhaps to use a washroom, perhaps because he was still dizzy from the lecturer's hold on his head. He entered a very small room or cell. The walls were old and covered with graffiti. A single, naked light-bulb hung down as a source of light. Reaching down into his trousers he examined his scrotum. He felt his testicles and found with them in his scrotum a third one and a forth. Then a voice said flatly and with objective intonation: "The God of the Christian religion is no god at all." Over and over again the voice repeated the statement: "The God of the Christian religion is no god at all." He thought it important to remember the statement.

Beside him on the floor there was some cheap newsprint-quality paper. With a pen he started to write down the sentence — "The God of the Christian religion . . ." — but before he could write the whole sentence down the earliest words began to vanish. The paper wouldn't take the ink. Again he tried to write the sentence down. Again and again, repetitively, compulsively. But the ink would not take. He noticed, however, that as he wrote the paper became of finer and finer quality until, at last, it attained a satin finish. Worried that he was going mad and that he would not be able to find his way out of the little closet (or even record the sentence that might hold the key to releasing him), he awoke with a fright.

After hearing a lecture on the Romantics, after hearing how Wordsworth tapped the hiding places of power for the refreshment of his soul's life, the dreamer finds himself in the yard outside St. Paul's Anglican Church even as Coleridge, in *The Rime of the Ancient Mariner,* let himself slip "below the Kirk, below the hill, below the lighthouse top" to the wellsprings of the creative imagination. When the dreamer resides outside the Church among his Gnostic brethren in the "vale of Soul-making," there is money in the grass, loose change. In the "vale of Soul-making," in that place of a salvation grander than that of the "chrysteain religion," change is loosed and value freed from the sacramental containers of the Church.

Inside the lecture hall, the contents of the dreamer's head push out even as the lecturer's hands squeeze in around it and tighten the focus. The pressure in the dreamer's head builds up like the multiplication of the loose change in the grass and makes him dizzy. He swoons and nearly passes out. The Romantic vision of the possibilities of soul-making is releasing his soul from its Christian parameters. An article titled "Elegy" catches the dreamer's attention. The lecturer is reciting an elegy. He is releasing the imagination by announcing the death of its old containers: the Christian Church and the Christian God.

The soul's release is the feminine's return. The female custodians step out of their janitorial roles, enter the Academy, and listen to the talk. Their release from patriarchal domination is what soul-making is all about. A fundamental taboo of totemism has been removed. The lecturer and the dark woman go off together as equals.

In the middle of the whole process, the dreamer leaves the lecture hall and, in a small cell or closet covered with the genital grammar (graffiti) of patriarchy, takes down his trousers and examines his testicles. There are four of them. Unlike Abraham's servant who placed his hand under Abraham's thigh to swear a solemn oath upon the patriarch's testicles (Gen. 24:2), the dreamer places his hand under his own thigh. The whole covenantal tradition, the whole tradition of projecting and reifying inhibited creativity, is collapsing into his scrotum. Money in the grass, pressure in the head, a doubling of the testicles: each image is a commentary on the others. No longer are there testicles above him. The testicles of God, like the tablets of Moses, have smashed to pieces like loose change in the grass. The soul has been released from the reified, codified, authorized traditions of the spirit into the multiple and individual possibilities of the imagination and soul-making. Like Aphrodite-Venus emerging from the severed testicles of the sky-father, Uranus, the female custodians and the dark woman emerge also. Charwomen are now sages.

"The God of the Christian religion is no god at all." The sentence is a declaration of freedom — freedom from the genital grammar of monotheistic tyranny. Any God who takes the imagination captive is not a god at all.

He tries to write the sentence down but he cannot. The ink will not take. Again and again he tries. He worries that he is going mad. Without God, without over-arching authority and limiting structures, there is uncertainty. Anything is possible. Perhaps, he thinks, simply writing down the declaration that the God is no god will give him a point of certainty, a standpoint. But soul-making will not be reified into final judgements and last words. The new wine will not be placed in the old bottles. With every sentence that will not take to the page, the dreamer is further abandoned to the process of writing and the uncertainties of the imagination (the question "What does the soul want?" [19]). Again and again he tries to write down a positive declaration, and each time the sentence vanishes. Over time, however, the paper transforms, becoming of finer and finer quality. The dreamer's soul, by long apprenticeship to uncertainty, coagulates into the substantiality and quality of satin-finish paper. It is precisely this process of interminable writing or soul-making that is the dreamer's way of stepping over the threshold of the reified trauma and into his own creative possibilities.

## The Pleasure of Dis-carnation

In the body, where Freud located the pleasure principle, pleasure means instinctual satisfaction, the release of pent-up physical tensions, drive reduction. In the spirit, where vicarious theology locates the pleasure principle, pleasure means belief in supernatural consolations and the futurity of an illusion. It is not necessary, however, to define pleasure solely in terms of the body or of the spirit. Pleasure need not be restricted to the discharge of instinctual dynamisms, an orgasm to end all orgasms, an apocalyptic rapture, or a gospel to end all gospels. Experienced within the perspective of the realm between body and spirit, the realm of soul or metaphor, pleasure is simply an aesthetic response, a breathing in,[20] a saving of the phenomena (rather than a reifying into physical or spiritual categories), a process with no end point.

In *The Ego and the Id*, Freud discusses how when "satisfaction triumphs . . . Eros is eliminated, and the death instinct has a free hand for accomplishing its purposes."[21] Freud illustrates his point by referring to the fact that the praying mantis and the drone bee die immediately after copulation. The literalization of instinct and pleasure into an energy model answerable to the law of entropy culminates finally in the reduction of all tension, "nirvana," and death. As noted by Rollo May, at this point in his reflections (*Beyond the Pleasure Principle*), Freud introduced the concept of Eros, a life-force that opposes the death-drive by introducing "fresh tensions."[22]

Like the Gnostic writer to whom the Docetist vision of Christ's transfiguration was revealed, Freud's vision of Eros was a Docetist transfiguration of his earlier, physiologically literalized (incarnational) conception of the Id and the pleasure principle. While down in the Jerusalem of a merely carnal intelligence a praying mantis and a drone bee were being crucified by the climax of corporeal satisfaction, up in a cave on the Mount of Olives, Eros, the pleasure principle in its subtle, metaphorical sense, was being revealed to Freud.

### Ordinary Unhappiness

From the beginning of his work as an analyst, Freud was modest about what could be achieved in the consulting room. Conveying this in the last paragraph of *Studies in Hysteria*, he draws upon the device of a fanciful conversation with an imagined patient. "Why," his patient remarks, "you tell me yourself that my illness is probably connected with my circumstances and the events of my life. You cannot alter these in any way. How do you propose to help me, then?" To this challenging query, Freud replies, "No doubt fate would find it easier than I do to relieve you of your illness. But you will be able to convince yourself that much will be gained if we succeed in transforming your hysterical misery into ordinary unhappiness." [23]

For all his work with his patients on their individuation or self-realization process, Jung said something very similar. In *The Psychology of the Transference*, he writes: "Like the alchemical end product, which always betrays its essential duality, the united personality will never quite lose the painful sense of innate discord. Complete redemption from the sufferings of this world is and must remain an illusion. Christ's earthly life likewise ended, not in complacent bliss, but on the cross." [24]

Psychotherapy, in the wake of Freud and Jung, has often lost sight of the sober realism of these founding practitioners, succumbing to what they both decried as the *furor sanandi*, the rage to heal. This is especially so when supplicants of its services have presented their suffering plaintively, with the absolute desperateness of lost souls. Seduced by the tendency of its patients' neuroses to take on a religious formulation and to demand cure in the most vicarious forms possible, psychotherapy has often fallen into hysterical collusion, regarding itself as a road to salvation. The human potentials movement has especially contributed to this suspect spiritualizing of psychotherapy. One has only to think of the agendas and goals of today's therapies. Are these not an embarrassment of riches: peak experiences, androgyny, individuation, wholeness, self-realization, nirvana, intimacy, transparency, love, assertiveness, mysticism, mind/body unity, left brain/right brain coherence, self-actualization, growth, happiness, etc?

The problem with ideal goals is that they are often nothing more than transcendental denials of the very difficulties which have occasioned interest in them in the first place. [25] Why all this fervor, numinosity, and missionary zeal? What is all this religious kitsch attempting to cover?

The English analyst Masud Khan has observed that it is not so difficult to cure a neurosis (as Freud concedes to his imagined patient, life could almost look after this by itself), no, the difficult thing is to cure a cure. The cure that Khan refers to here is the patient's anxiety-avoiding, reality-denying, and often addictive self-cure. [26] In a similar formulation, Jung defined neurosis as a substitute for the necessary and legitimate suffering that we all must reckon with in life. [27]

But let us return to that embarrassment of riches that psychotherapy gives rise to as it acts out in the spirit its inability to make room in the soul for what life brings. In an early conversation, Freud admonished Jung that they must erect "an unshakable bulwark... against the black tide of mud... of occultism." [28] Withstanding the urge to meet its patients' sometimes very trippy desires for salvation with hypnotic, faith-healing spin of its own, therapy, in keeping with Freud's concern, must pull the rug out from under the *false* spirituality by which the so-called flight into health is so often pursued in our day.

An attentive disinterestedness, workaday steadiness, and caring neutrality in the therapist can bring to therapy a sobering counterweight to the patient's tendency to zealously transfer and identify with ideals that are little more than whitewashed versions of his difficulties. The attitudes of "cool benevolence" and "benign indifference" — so characteristic of Freud — can, like the voice of Daedalus, help restrain the flights of those patients who, like Icaros, would fly too near to those sunny illusions that are nothing more than inverted versions of the very symptoms they believe they are recovering from, i.e., the Gods they have made of their inhibitions and traumas, obsessions, and fetishes.

To many the unpretentious aim of returning people to "ordinary unhappiness" will seem too modest. After all, there is more to life than "ordinary unhappiness." It may be argued, however, that this "more" should be left to the patient to find, or rather, to make — in concert with the therapist. Bearing in mind that disillusionment is what brings us to reality, patient and therapist must learn to try their inspirations, re-frames, and cohering fables, much as John taught the faithful that they must try the spirits to ascertain which were of God (1 John 4:1). They must, that is to say, be mindful of the tendency of the patient's spiritual flights to simply transcend and bypass the challenge of the soul and its making.

## Dreams

What is the "right" dream interpretation? When one is held in thrall by the Trauma-God, the "right" interpretation is the one that kills that God and releases the creative power displaced on Him back into human hands, back into the hands of the dreamer.

Too often dream interpretation degenerates into vicarious religion. Many Jungians of the classical school, for instance, consider dreams to be messages from what they call the empirical god-image, the archetype of the Self. According to this point of view, dreams tell us what to do, or at least, how to adjust our one-sided ego-attitudes. Many Freudians, on the other hand, believe with Freud that the purpose of dreams is to protect sleep from the vicissitudes of the instincts by sating them with images. Following upon this, Freudian analysis looks to the dream to provide information relevant to the development of the libido. When the "dreamwork" is untangled by the work of interpretation, the patient is confronted with his infantile fixations and encouraged to sublimate them into more mature forms of expression.

The same can be said of most schools of psychology. Across the board, the dream is approached on the basis of meta-psychological models of psychic structure that are taken literally. These models, however, are conjectures which posit the psyche and the dream beyond the reach of man's creating will. Propitiating traumatic factors, their tendency is to regard the psyche's images as secondarily reflecting more substantial realities such as instinct, the breast, the letter in the unconscious, the family system, sexuality, early infant development or some other privileged sphere or God-term. The primacy of imagination, its role in creating our reality-sense (as it reflects all things into themselves), goes unrecognized in these approaches.

Now, I am not merely saying with Korzybski that the map is not the territory. More than that, I am saying that what territory there is is always already a function of our cartography. It is we who are the "divine" artificers, we who are the makers of what is humanly real (notwithstanding that our characters can get away on us!).

This is not to deny that life in its immensity can be overpowering. Nor is it to overlook the fact that we are utterly dependent on many things. Lord knows, it can be difficult to hold our own, the contingencies of existence being what they are! Our dreams, however, can sometimes turn the tables, if only by exercising an imaginative power that is as crazily creative as the traumas of our lives are obdurate and determining. Is this why dreams have traditionally been regarded as being given by the divine?

It happens every night. Torn from their physical, Newtonian setting, impressions borrowed from the day appear to us in a strange, decontextualized manner. Examining these images we find that we cannot be sure if they even represent themselves — the objects they seem to be modelled upon. It seems, to the contrary, that they are free of such referents now; no longer images *of* this, that, or the other thing but *as* these things — images *per se*. [29]

So decontextualized are the images that the dreams utilize that it should be possible, theoretically at least, to create anything with them. Is it against this possibility that we erect the orthodoxies of interpretation? "I fear," wrote Nietzsche, "that we are not getting rid of God because we still believe in grammar." [30] Today, *post mortem dei*, should we not share a similar concern for what one analytical psychologist, bringing God and grammar together in relation to the dream, has called "God's forgotten language"? [31]

In addition to his fear about God living on in our grammar, Nietzsche had another related concern. Casting a worried eye toward the future, he rued the day "when man will no longer launch the arrow of his longing beyond man — and the string of his bow will have unlearned how to whizz." [32] Here, again, is a hint about how best to approach the dream. Drawing back its bowstring as far as it can, interpretation should arrow the images of each dream well beyond our operative consciousness. Ever taunt, it should take the battle to that enemy — be it a trauma, a God-term, or a theory — that would render its meanings rote.

The "right" interpretation is the most daring interpretation that a disciplined hermeneutic can allow. Original and originating, it is like a new precedent in the law: Mr. Smith versus the State of California; Mr. Jones versus Freud and Jung. Or moving from court room to launching pad (even as dreams are so liable to scene changes), interpretation may be likened to the space project of an ever-opening consciousness. Imagined in the light of this image, the ideas arising out if it are the heaven-storming rockets and space-probes of that creating will called man.

Art or Life

An art critic dreamt that he and his wife were at the foot of the cross where Christ hung crucified. Although they were together in the scene, even as they are a couple in actual life, they were very differently positioned within it. Specifically, while he stood on a mat of split bamboo a short remove from Christ, his wife stood closer, writhing in agony as she watched the nailed feet of Jesus twist in pain. In an aside to his wife the dreamer asked, "Do you think we should take this aesthetically or humanly?"

The question is a telling one, not only for the dreamer personally but for our times. For over two thousand years the passion of Christ has symbolically yoked the aesthetic and the human together, inspiring artistic and cultural productivity on a grand scale. But here, in this dream, the both/and-ness of the previously effective symbol has become the either/or of a post-Christian ennui, while, at the same time, the trauma that the symbol had mediated and shielded us from breaks through again — at least for the anima-figure who feels it so intensely.

The dreamer's stance in the dream, both with respect to the cross and with respect to his wife, reiterates his question. His standpoint is an aesthetic one, the flexible mat of split bamboo. The wife, meanwhile, has as her standpoint the nailed feet of the crucified Christ. She feels the agony of the Lord whereas her dispassionate husband does not. Evidently, the relationship between the aesthetic and the human, the pleasure and reality principles, art and life, image and affect, husband and wife, God and man is being unconsciously interrogated out of tension occasioned by a dissociative split. As presented by the dream, the relationship between these pairs is like the relationship between the dream-ego and the dream-wife who are standing askew in front of a more traumatically vivid version of the crucifix than the one the dreamer and his wife actually stood before many years ago when they were first married.

Now marriage in our day, even when backed by the sacred standard of Christ's marriage to his Church (or possibly *because* it has so long had such vicarious support) has increasingly lost its strength as an institution. We need only think of the ubiquity of separation and divorce. In contrast to the Christ who so courageously embraced "the marriage bed of the Cross," few today so resolutely embrace the cross of marriage. Reflecting upon the dream with these thoughts in mind, we might wonder if the dreamer would get on better with his anima without benefit of clergy. Perhaps the aesthetic and the human, as well as the other pairs we listed, would enact a *coniuntio* better fitted to our times outside the Church. Perhaps art, pushing off from the inspiration it once received from Christianity, must become post-Christian (as I am sure it has now been for more than a century) if it is again to confront the traumatic contingencies to which humanity is subject and to provide a container for events and experiences which might otherwise prove unabsorbable — even for theology. Coming at this another way, we need not look far to see how gutless, disembodied, and effete art becomes when it absolutizes itself as an aesthetic and loses its connection to its stigmatic source in human pain and passion.

Since the dream we are examining has imaged the relationship between the aesthetic, the human, and the divine through the metaphor of the couple and their Kierkegaardian "Either/Or" marriage, it is important to free our reflections from the sentimentalities to which the marriage image has become attached. Heaven is a married land, according to the New Testament. In *The Revelation to John*, Christ marries the city, New Jerusalem, which descends out of heaven "as a bride adorned to meet her bridegroom." In the more laicized terms of the popular imagination it is commonly said that "marriage is made in heaven." But is it not precisely vicarious thinking of this kind that severs the aesthetic and the human into the dissociated extremes of bamboo and crucifixion? Is this not another example of a conjecturing that has reached beyond man's own creating will? When the soul has been made "an honest woman of" by vicarious religion, when the dream-wife is transfixed by the spectacle of God's humanity in Christ's (for us) vicarious suffering, its pain, we may suspect, has become romantically inflated, and its husband, the cuckolded aesthetic impulse (the impulse to soul-making), reduced to conceptual bamboo reasonings. And all this is to say nothing of Mel Gibson's attempt bail out the spiritually bankrupt West by taking out a second mortgage on Christ's passion by means of a Hollywood blockbuster! Watching that fascist send-up there can be no doubt that the blood of Christ's sacrifice — which Gibson spills so abundantly for the camera — has lost much of its effectiveness.

## Nuclear Escalation

Nuclear arms, world-destroying power in the hands of man, can be viewed as a transitional stage between vicarious religion and soul-making. With nuclear weapons man swallows God; man becomes his own God, his own danger, his own trauma. With nuclear arms man releases himself from the vicarious supports of religion. No longer can he conceive of himself in a covenantal relationship with an omnipotent God. No longer can he look away from his own power and responsibility to the power and responsibility he projects into God. Grace has become extinct in the nuclear age.

At a certain point in the cold war between the United States and the Soviet Union, at a certain point in the stockpiling of nuclear weapons, the magnitude of God was transcended. Today our creative power, our destructive power, exceeds the power we have displaced onto God. No longer does the God of man's conjecturing reach beyond the power of man's own creating will.

God *was* big, even as the First and Second World Wars were big. It took the systematic extermination of millions of Jews, Poles, Japanese, homosexuals and Gypsies — not to mention the soldiers who died in action — for mankind to feel anything. Only when our human tragedy had become slightly larger than the capacity of our religious containers to absorb it were we able to *experience* our humanity. Ironically, with the death camps and the bomb, man gave himself back to himself.

The twentieth-century stockpile of nuclear arms is bigger than God. Today we can feel the burden of our creative/destructive power. Individuating a relationship to our immense power involves the global community in a tremendous world of soul-making. A renaissance is enacting itself today in terms of the escalation and de-escalation of the arms race.

In 1944 Jung could still write that, "Despite appearances to the contrary, the establishment of order and the dissolution of what has been established are at bottom beyond human control." If today we can no longer share Jung's conviction on this point it is because, as Jung writes in his next sentence, we are now aware that "... only that which can destroy itself is truly alive." [33]

Deliver Us From Salvation

It was once believed by many that the rewards of the spirit come from good works. But the idea that heaven could be purchased by good behavior contained an even more fundamental idea — the idea that God could be paid off with protection money. Religion degenerated into a kind of insurance policy. Priests, like indemnity underwriters of a mafia godfather, sold sow's ear indulgences to their parishioners who wanted to sin without compromising their places in heaven. Luther, appalled by this salvation-mongering, argued that we are justified not by good works or sow's ears but by faith. God, for Luther, could not be bought or sold, nor could salvation. Faith in God, alone, he held to be the prerequisite for salvation, and faith was entirely God's gift.

The notion of salvation is eternally corruptible. The priest can wholesale it, and Calvin can go to the opposite extreme and argue that it is doled out by the whim of a stingy God to an elect few. Indeed, each denomination has fostered allegiance to itself through its teachings about salvation. But how many theological hairs will have to be split before we realize that what we need salvation from is the very notion of salvation itself? Soul-making burns the salvific bridge that theology would erect between the sacred and the profane, this world and the next. In soul-making we are justified neither by good works nor by spiritual election but, rather, by fiction. "The images that yet/fresh images beget" is the only salvation soul-making offers. How we dramatize ourselves to ourselves, how the soul imagines our lives, how we dream events into experiences — that is what justifies the anti-salvation that is soul-making. Grounding in fiction, in life as fiction, saves us from the fantasy (which forgets it is a fantasy) of a life-transcending, saving truth. We make soul by releasing it from the pretensions of a salvation that would save it.

1. Willis Barnstone, ed., *The Other Bible* (New York: Harper & Row, 1984), p. 419.

2, Sigmund Freud, "Mourning and Melancholia," in *CP* 4: 154.

3. Cited in Henri Corbin, "Divine Epiphany and Spiritual Birth in Ismailian Gnosis," in *Man and Transformation*, ed. J. Campbell, Papers from the Eranos Yearbooks, vol. 5, 2nd ed. (Princeton: Princeton University Press, 1972), p. 69.

4. *The Other Bible*, p. 420.

5. Sigmund Freud, *The Future of an Illusion*, trans. W.D. Robson-Scott (New York: Doubleday Anchor, 1964), p. 30.

6. Ibid., p. 31.

7. C.G. Jung, *CW* 8: 336.

8. Billie Holiday, "God Bless the Child."

9. C.G. Jung, *CW* 5: 655.

10. Sigmund Freud, "The Passing of the Oedipus complex," *CP* 2: 273.

11. C.G. Jung, *CW* 7: 88.

12. C.G. Jung, *CW* 6: 373f.

13. C.G. Jung, *C.G. Jung Speaking: Interviews and Encounters*, ed. W. McGuire and R.F.C. Hull (Princeton: Princeton University Press, 1977), p. 359.

14. C.G. Jung *CW* 10: 367.

15. Cited in Jeffrey Moussieff Masson, *The Assault on Truth: Freud's Suppression of the Seduction Theory* (New York: Viking Penguin, 1985), pp. 108-109.

16. Ibid..

17. Wallace Stevens, *The Palm at the End of the Mind*, ed. Holly Stevens (New York: Vintage Books, 1972), pp. 253–54.

18. John Keats, *Selected Poems and Letters*, ed. D. Bush (Boston: Houghton Mifflin, 1958), p. 288.

19. Cf. James Hillman, *Healing Fiction* (Barrytown, NY: Station Hill, 1983), pp. 85–129.

20. Cf. James Hillman, "Anima Mundi: The Return of the Soul to the World," in *Spring 1982*: 80.

21. Cited by Rollo May, *Love and Will* (New York: Dell Publishing, 1969), p. 86.

22. Ibid., p. 85.

23. Sigmund Freud & Josef Breuer, *Studies on Hysteria*, trans. J. Strachey (New York: Basic Books, 1957), p. 305. Translation slightly modified.

24. C.G. Jung, *CW* 16: 400.

25, Cf. James Hillman on the transcendental denial of pathologizing in his *Re-Visioning Psychology*, pp. 64–67.

26. Masud Khan, *The Privacy of the Self* (New York: International Universities Press, 1974), p. 97.

27. C.G. Jung, CW II: 129.

28. C.G. Jung, *Memories, Dreams, Reflections*, A. Jaffe, ed., R. and C. Winston, trans. (New York: Pantheon, 1963), p. 150.

29. For more on the image *of* / image *as* distinction see James Hillman, "Further Notes on Images," *Spring 1978*: 173.

30. Friedrich Nietzsche, *The Twilight of the Idols; The Anti-Christ*, trans. R.J. Hollingdale (Harmondsworth: Penguin Books, 1968), p. 38.

31. John A. Sanford, *God's Forgotten Language*, (J.B. Lippincott Co., 1968).

32. Friedrich Nietzsche, *The Philosophy of Nietzsche* (New York: The Modern Libary, 1927), p. 11.

33. C.G. Jung CW 12: 93.

# chapter three

REPEATING, IMAGINING, AND MAKING A CRUST

## The Crust Around the Pleasure Principle

The chaos of beginnings. Atoms and the void. Expanding out from the
BIG BANG — planets, stars, and chemical processes. The tumult at the
back of things. Lava flows. The gloom of Tartarus. Dionysus born of his
own dismemberment. The risen Christ, "slain from the foundations of
the world" (Rev. 13:8). The whole of creation progressing deathward to
no death. The eerie tones of oboes, kettle drums, and strings. Stravinsky's
*Le Sacre du Printemps* already performing itself tens of millennia before
any men, let alone Stravinsky, had yet appeared. Origins building upon
themselves; a glacial ballet. Tensions arising and then falling back again,
but not as far back as the time before. Boulder giants and frost demons.
Negentropy and the crash of thunder. Shafts of lightning. The illumined
redness of tooth and claw. And also nature's light. The associative thinking that is already there in things, in their likeness to one another, in the
found alphabet of the letters that they are. Distinctions, comparisons,
nuances; qualities, differences, reflexivities. A tree branch sounding in
the forest as it falls. But not without the mediating layer, more dead than
living — the bark of the tree, the exoskeleton of the insect, the character
of the ego — that protects and provides for the sentience of the more
delicate layers tucked away behind them . . .

Redolent of the buffeting forces from which it has dialectically
emerged, life, in Freud's view, has as its most basic tropism or instinct
a compulsive urge to restore the preceding state of things. Now, since
the earliest of all states was that of lifeless, inorganic matter, Freud regarded the repetition compulsion (present clinically in such phenomena
as a patient's mimicking of events that have traumatized him) to be an
expression of a death instinct. In his discussion of this radical notion, the
great analyst-mythmaker posed the question, "But how is the predicate
of being 'instinctual' related to the compulsion to repeat?" His answer,
so important for our reflections on trauma, immediately follows:

At this point we cannot escape a suspicion that we may have come upon the track of a universal attribute of instincts and perhaps of organic life in general . . . *It seems, then, that an instinct is an urge inherent in organic life to restore an earlier state of things* which the living entity has been obliged to abandon under the pressure of external disturbing forces; that is, it is a kind of organic elasticity, or, to put it in another way, the expression of the inertia inherent in organic life. [1]

Originally, primordially, what later came to be known as instinct was very close to the inorganic matter from which life emerged, so close, in fact, that Freud defined the instincts as a conservative tendency to restore earlier situations, the lifeless state of inorganic matter being the earliest of all. Freud attributes the fact that complex life forms have developed despite this tendency to "the pressure of external disturbing forces," which have made the path to death and the inorganic state of things more and more circuitous:

The attributes of life were at some time evoked in inanimate matter by the action of a force of whose nature we can form no conception. It may perhaps have been a process similar in type to that which later caused the development of consciousness in a particular stratum of living matter. The tension which then arose in what had hitherto been an inanimate substance endeavored to cancel itself out. In this way the first instinct came into being: the instinct to return to the inanimate state. It was still an easy matter at that time for a living substance to die; the course of its life was probably only a brief one, whose direction was determined by the chemical structure of the young life. For a long time, perhaps, living substance was thus being constantly created afresh and easily dying, till decisive external influences altered in such a way as to oblige the still surviving substance to diverge ever more widely from its original course of life and to make even more complicated *détours* before reaching its aim of death. These circuitous paths to death, faithfully kept to by the conservative instincts, would thus present us today with the picture of the phenomena of life. If we firmly maintain the exclusively conservative nature of instincts, we cannot arrive at any other notions as to the origins and aim of life. [2]

After pursuing this line of thought to its extreme, Freud then rel-
ativizes it by introducing the idea of another set of instincts to which
can be attributed "an internal impulse towards 'progress' and towards
higher development!" [3] These are the sexual or life instincts. While the
death instinct seeks to return to the state of inanimate matter, the sexual
instincts "repeat the performance to which [organisms] owe their existence," that is, they repeat "the beginning process of development." [4]

> [The sexual instincts] are conservative in the same sense as the
> other instincts in that they bring back earlier states of living
> substance; but they are conservative to a higher degree in that
> they are peculiarly resistant to external influences; and they
> are conservative too in another sense in that they preserve life
> itself for a comparatively long period. They are the true life
> instincts. They operate against the purpose of the other in-
> stincts, which leads, by reason of their function, to death; and
> this fact indicates that there is an opposition between them and
> the other instincts, an opposition whose importance was long
> ago recognized by the theory of the neuroses. It is as though
> the life of the organism moved with a vacillating rhythm. One
> group of instincts rushes forward so as to reach the final aim of
> life as swiftly as possible; but when a particular stage in the ad-
> vance has been reached, the other group jerks back to a certain
> point to make a fresh start and so prolong the journey. [5]

Although the life and death instincts oppose one another, there is
a sense in which the partial success of the death instinct facilitates life.
Freud asks us to "picture a living organism in its most simplified possible
form as an undifferentiated vesicle of a substance that is susceptible to
stimulation." [6] The outer surface of this vesicle, the surface bordering
on the external world, becomes altered by the impingement of external
stimuli upon it. At some point, the outer surface, permanently changed
by external influences, reaches a limit beyond which further modification is impossible. "A crust would thus be formed which would at last
have been so thoroughly 'baked through' by stimulation that it would
present the most favorable possible conditions for the reception of stimuli and become incapable of any further modification." [7] It is this "crust"
or "shield," this dead zone of organic matter that has returned to an

inorganic state, that both protects the living substance inside it and makes it possible for that living matter to have consciousness of the external world. "By its death," writes Freud,

> the outer layer has saved all the deeper ones from a similar fate — unless, that is to say, stimuli reach it which are so strong that they break through the protective shield. *Protection against* stimuli is an almost more important function for the living organism than *reception of* stimuli . . . The main purpose of the *reception* of stimuli is to discover the direction and nature of the external stimuli; and for that it is enough to take small specimens of the external world, to sample it in small quantities. [8]

Stated negatively, the repetition compulsion is an instinctual process of an entirely retrograde nature, a defense against the vicissitudes of the inorganic world wrought through identification with the inorganic world — a partial dying. Stated positively, the repetition compulsion is a *post hoc* attempt to thicken the skin, bake the crust, or harden the shield which protects the life inside. Viewed in this later perspective, traumatic dreams (as well as other psychological phenomena that do not operate in terms of the pleasure principle) "are endeavoring to master the stimulus retrospectively, by developing the anxiety whose omission was the cause of the traumatic neurosis." [9]

## Nietzsche's Body

When Nietzsche proclaimed God to be dead, he punctured the "crust" mankind had baked around itself, which protected it from the vicissitudes of the inorganic world. Just as the outer layer of any living organism is *supposed to be dead* in order to protect the living organism from excess stimulation and to provide the limitations necessary if there is to be consciousness, theology is supposed to be dead — rigid, contrived, defensive, dogmatic — in order to fulfil its function.

Theology stands as a shield between mankind and trauma. A compromise with the trauma, theology is a return of our exterior surfaces to the inorganic world, that is, to the spiritual world, death.

To operate optimally, to protect mankind adequately, religion must be a dead shell — mere lip-service, Sabbath after Sabbath, mere duty. The Christianity of Bismarck's Germany, the Christianity Nietzsche so hated, was a buttress of health and protection in this sense.

But Nietzsche courted higher altitudes and stronger sensations. He was not content with the stimulation that filtered through the scales and armored plates of Christianity, the death-in-life religion. He did not want to be a creature deadening his surfaces in a salvific compromise with the wholly other creator. He wanted to be a creator in his own right, more fully than had ever before been dared.

Referring to himself as both "the physiologist" and the "first psychologist of Christianity," Nietzsche sought to tap the ruptures of Christianity's protective shell for a philosophy of the most intense stimuli. Nietzsche's philosophy is, as he himself called it, a philosophy of convalescence. In an act of super-abundant strength, Nietzsche sloughed off his protective Christian skin and stood exposed before the stimuli that the dead faith had helped to filter.

Nietzsche was a philosopher of trauma. By renouncing the benevolent protection of a dead God, he laid himself open to the "divine influx" of the powers that the dead God helped to keep at bay precisely through being dead. His personal ailments — his migraine, his phlegm, his syphilis — he raised to this meaning.

Nietzsche was forever talking about becoming harder and colder. His intellect was a robust body which could tolerate more and more arduous sensations and freedoms. By surrendering his culture's armor of dead theology and exposing himself to what he called many "little deaths," Nietzsche sought to become both sensitive and hard at the same time.

In Nietzsche, perception no longer dwelt behind a thick defensive layer of outer death. The act of perception, for him, was an aggressive act, an act of willing, inventing and making that developed its own rugged skin (and renounced it) as it proceeded. "There are many souls," wrote Nietzsche, "that one will never discover unless one invents them first." [10]

The doctrine of eternal recurrence plays a similar role in Nietzsche's traumatic philosophy as the repetition compulsion plays in Freud's theory of traumatic neuropathology. Just as repetition is a way of retrospectively mastering an overwhelming influx of stimuli by developing the anxiety whose omission was the cause of the traumatic neurosis, eternal recurrence was Nietzsche's way of mastering the stimuli released through his trauma-courting rejection of Christianity's protective crust — the incarnation and its millennialist sense of history. By eternalizing every act and moment of his own life, by inflating his every action into the cosmological proportions of the original creation, Nietzsche sought to condition himself to the burden of his own existence. Nietzsche felt that if he could commit himself to his every creative act as if it had always been and would always recur, he could replace the protective shield of dead theology with the hard muscle of his own creating will. Eros and Thanatos, the life and death instincts, would then no longer be opposed; rather, the two forces would be subsumed under another drive, the will-to-power, the making of one's own life and death and soul.

## Sunday Reverie

Sabbath after Sabbath we "act out what we cannot remember" and attempt to "master the [overwhelming] stimulus retrospectively, by developing the anxiety whose omission was the cause of the traumatic neurosis" [11] we call our religion. The job of religion is to fill us with the fear of the Lord — guilt, remorse, sin, and fear — that we might better face the traumas that overwhelmed our ancestors. The faithful are "obliged to *repeat* the repressed material as a contemporary experience [i.e., worship and ritual] instead of, as the physician would prefer to see, *remembering* it as something belonging to the past." [12]

## Crust-Making

The tortoise in its shell, the fish in its scales, the rhinoceros in its hide — all creatures great and small — live by virtue of a protective outer crust of dead matter. The purpose of this protective crust or shield, according to Freud, is for "*protection against* stimuli." [13] The shells, scales, skins, and furry hides function as extremely selective perceptual windows or filters, editing out the greater part of the "enormous energies at work in the external world." As Freud writes:

> The main purpose of the *reception* of stimuli is to discover the direction and nature of the external stimuli; and for that it is enough to take small specimens of the external world, to sample it in small quantities. [14]

Soul-making is the human refinement of the crust-making process, which is present in all living beings. Human beings, no less than other creatures, are beings with skins, crusts, shells, and hides. I am not just thinking of the history of what mankind has clothed itself in — the animal skins, shirts of mail, hoop skirts, corsets, jock-straps, mini-skirts, polyester suits, designer jeans, space uniforms, and bikini swim wear. I am thinking also of language and metaphor. Men and women live in their metaphors as a tortoise lives in its shell or an animal in its hide. The difference between the person we call "thick-skinned" and the person we call "thin-skinned" may be a function of the ways each dramatizes himself to himself. Whether a potential hurt rolls off us "like water off a duck's back" or flays us alive depends in large measure on the metaphors and analogies we filter it through. To the extent that I can associate the "arrows and slings of outrageous fortune," which befall me to precedents in a text, a work of literature, or a popular saying, I will be protected from the raw immensity of that stimuli and, yet, be able to "sample it in small quantities."

Man, in his subtle body, is the most chameleon of all creatures. Faster than the agamid lizard can change its color and disappear against the foliage, the "naked ape," Man, can change his metaphors. The significance of Man's chameleonic capacity becomes clear when we compare him with creatures with extremely thick and inflexible crusts. The oyster, for instance, living on the ocean floor in its rugged shell, is so protected from the stimuli of the external world that the life inside is without a head. Receptive to an extremely narrow band of stimuli, oysters do not see, taste, or smell. Man's capacity to change his skin, shift his metaphors, and wear a variety of garments protects him in a fashion that allows him to sample more of the stimuli emanating from the external world than any other creature. How unlike an oyster's shell is John Donne's metaphor "like gold to airy thinness beat."

Given that Man owes the evolution of his sentient nervous system to his capacity to protect himself with subtler and subtler skins and linguistic distinctions (metaphors), it is not surprising that in his aesthetics he should value those same qualities. The thinnest porcelain, the most lightweight winter jacket, the slinkiest bikini, the most delicate poem: behind the making of each of these artifacts (though in a restrained fashion), is Shelley's urge to break the imagination's "dome of many-colored glass" to expose "the white radiance of Eternity."

This brings us back to trauma. As a refining of the dead crusts that protect us, soul-making is an attempt to experience more and more of the traumatic stimuli emanating from the world external to us. It is a precarious process of refining sensitivity and perception. Ever and again the temptation is to smash the imagination's dome, go out in to the wintry day in too lightweight a coat, or to lie on the sunny beach too long. Or going the other way, the temptation may be to step up the defensive function of the skin. Today, at a time in history when the world's most powerful nations are devoting so much of their attention and resources to global-reach defense activity, the danger for the soul is that the shield may get so thick that closure results. Like the rugged shell of an oyster, such efforts as former president Reagan's proposed "Strategic Defense Initiatives" and George W. Bush's "Missile Defense Shield" could well facilitate an atrophying of man's nervous system. Like the oyster in its shell, Man could find himself losing his head.

Like these totalized defense strategies, vicarious religion protects the soul so absolutely from exposure to events that the soul shrivels up for lack of stimulation. The black and white splitting, the reversal of murder into sacrifice and the subsequent identification with the aggressor, the displacement of all tribulation onto Christ, the dogma of original sin and its weekly confession — to say nothing of the hysterical conversion reactions — all result in such a blanket response to the challenge of existence that life is sampled in only the most minute dosages.

In what he took to be a "grander system of salvation than the chryste-ain religion," Keats, in his letter to his brother, argued for "Soul-making." Soul-making, for Keats, would be the refining of a particularized aware-ness. Though there may by "sparks of divinity in millions . . . they are not Souls till they acquire identities, till each one is personally itself."

> I[n]telligences are atoms of perception — they know and they see and they are pure, in short, they are God — How then are Souls to be made? How then are these sparks which are God to have identity given them — so as ever to possess a bliss peculiar to each one's individual existence? [15]

Thinner, finer, subtler and more complex: thus soul wants us. The awareness of the particularity of an individual existence is dependent upon relationship with other particulars. But if our skins are so com-posed that stimuli emanating from another being are levelled out into an amorphous mass of static, or if the skin around the other is similarly constituted, there will exist an insufficient context in terms of which to differentiate uniqueness. The stimuli will continue to be propitiated and preserved at the level of trauma; the "bliss peculiar to each one's indi-vidual existence" will not be sensed; the soul will not be made.

## Language, Crust, and Deconstruction

Those deconstructionists! What thick skins they have! Imagine the luxury of being able to assert that words are not a function of the ob-jects they seem to signify, but, rather, of their relationship to other words. When the psychotherapist reads these critics, he is filled with envy. If only his patients were so linguistically well-constituted. If only they could turn their projection-laden, referential communications into self-reflective texts. Like Socrates leading the slave-boy to recol-lect knowledge he did not know he had, the therapist helps his patients to see the connections between their words, hoping to free them of the blight of referents. If they could only realize that their symptoms are rhetorical, perhaps they would cease to vicariously ascribe blame and salvation to others.

The language spoken by a patient, however, is usually not the language of the text which the deconstructionist reads. The patient's fictions of himself are to literature what prose is to poetry and what life is to death. While the patient's language is a language of *living* referents, literature as literature is elegy, a language of *dead* referents. Poems, plays, and novels, as the deconstructionist critics rightly argue, are never about life. As a layer of dead referents, however, they may serve to protect the life we live in their midst. "This little fragment of living substance," writes Freud,

> is suspended in the middle of an external world charged with the most powerful energies; and it would be killed by the stimulation emanating from these if it were not provided with a protective shield against stimuli. It acquires the shield in this way: its outermost surface ceases to have the structure proper to living matter, becomes to some degree inorganic and thenceforward functions as a special envelope or membrane resistant to stimuli. In consequence, the energies of the external world are able to pass into the next underlying layers, which have remained living, with only a fragment of their original intensity; and these layers can devote themselves, behind the protective shield, to the reception of the amounts of stimulus which have been allowed through it. By its death, the outer layer has saved all the deeper ones from a similar fate — unless, that is to say, stimuli reach it which are so strong that they break through the protective shield ... The protective shield is supplied with its own store of energy and must above all endeavor to preserve the special modes of transformation of energy operating in it against the effects threatened by the enormous energies at work in the external world — effects which tend towards a levelling out of them and hence towards destruction. [16]

The histrionic speech acts of the patient point to the failure of literature. The free-associations, slips of the tongue, and reports of "what happened" are not the ravings of a Lear, the soliloquy of a Hamlet, or the story of an omniscient narrator, but, rather, seepage from the fissures

to bring about a savage re-doubling of the resistances and distrustful attacks upon rapport. If, however, the therapist is able to interpret these death-dealing dynamics while, at the same time, affirming the portion of life-instincts present in them, the patient's attempt to retrospectively develop the crust necessary to get on with the life that it is actually possible to have will be facilitated. No longer merely a protective armor of the self behind rigid character defenses, the crust becomes more complex and refined in its structure. As an organ of perception now, it is capable of subtler, more nuanced observations and insights.

Does this mean that what Freud called "the negative therapeutic reaction" is analyzable after all? Though by the time of his late paper, "Analysis Terminable and Interminable," Freud had become very pessimistic on this score, the views he put forward there (I am thinking specifically of those based on the dark vision of his *Beyond the Pleasure Principle*) provide a most valuable heuristic for listening and cure. [20] Just as the outer surface of a simple vesicle must die and return to the state of inorganic matter if it is to filter the stimuli reaching it from without in such a fashion that they may become accessible to consciousness, so the analytic couple must travail through much skulduggery if the patient's capacity to love and work is finally to die into life.

A presenting neurosis is one thing, the transference neurosis another. If the cure of a patient's presenting neurosis is not to be vicarious — a product, merely, of the seductions of suggestion — it must be approached analytically, that is, in the dark light of those elements of the transference neurosis that are beyond the pleasure principle. Said another way, before the patient can transform his presenting neurosis into "ordinary unhappiness," the destructive, havoc-seeking transference projections must be received and worked through. Where important insights and good rapport had earlier been negated by the so-called negative therapeutic reaction, these in turn may be negated again in what Hegel called the negation of the negation. The dead love of the properly handled transference will form a protective skin around the patient making it possible for the patient to love and work again. ". . . when a particular stage in the advance [of the death-instincts] has been reached," writes Freud, "the other group [i.e., the life-instincts] jerks back to a certain point to make

a fresh start . . ."[21] Able now to dignify the bitter-sweet intimacy of the
therapy by assuming the burden of his or her own life, the patient is free
to love and work again. Therapy has reached a satisfactory conclusion.

## Upside-Down

When a trauma has repeated itself many times, it loses its traumatic
quality. The compulsive propitiations become automatic; the ritualized
avoidances routine; the neurosis itself oddly comfortable.

When I was a child in school we did a science experiment. One of
the students wore a pair of glasses that reversed perception such that
the world appeared upside-down. After several days of constantly wearing these glasses and stumbling around in an upside-down world, the
boy's perception began to normalize. In spite of the distorting glasses,
the world again appeared to him right-side-up. The reverse of this was
just as interesting. When, after several days, the boy took off the glasses,
he was astonished to find that the world appeared upside-down to his
naked eyes. He was just as disoriented, nauseous and confused as he was
when he had first put on the distorting glasses. It took several days for
his perceptual system to adjust and for his picture of the world to turn
right-side-up again.

A trauma distorts our perceptions and turns our world upside-
down. For days, or months, or years we stumble around nauseous and
confused. Like the boy who wore the distorting glasses, we become hy-
per-vigilant. We scan the world for dangers while learning to use our
new eyes. Hesitantly, gingerly, reticently, neurotically we walk through
the world. (To outsiders all this can look like quite the opposite: staggering carelessness, self-abuse, histrionics, and hypomania.) Gradually,
however, our perceptual system accommodates to the traumatic distortion of reality. We become used to the inverting lenses of our negative
complexes. The nausea goes away. We find our comfort range. We know
where we can go and where we cannot. Our gingerly gait, which is at the
same time our staggering gait, comes to feel like our natural gait. Our

trauma-skewed perceptions become our home, and we live in them like an agoraphobic, only comfortable when we are "inside" them.

When a chronically neurotic patient, a patient who has long been habituated to his complexed perceptions, complains of anxiety attacks, nausea, or disorientation, it may be because the distorting glasses are coming off. When this is the case, and the traumatic complexes through which he has been perceiving the world misplace themselves, break, or simply wear out, the world appears in what seems at first a distorted and threatening aspect. Having become so accustomed to the convoluted perceptions of a traumatized consciousness, situations anomalous to the expectations of that consciousness — benign, non-noxious situations — seem frighteningly suspect. The patient feels he is getting worse. He feels a nausea or anxiety that he had not felt for years. Now, however, it is because he is getting better. The distorting glasses are simply coming off, and the world of mainstream reality that is returning from repression seems at first upset.

With my patients I sometimes do a countdown. "How many minutes did your anxiety attack last? Five minutes? In the whole week you've had only ten minutes? So in the last ten years you've had only a few days or a week of anxiety, only a few days or a week outside the complex?" When the glasses come off, it may take the patient some time to get used to "real life" again. "This week I want you to have more anxiety attacks if you can possibly manage it. When the glasses come off, leave them off. Don't pick up your bi-focals or your tri-focals. Expect to get a headache, a feeling of dizziness, a feeling of nausea. Make allowances for all that. It will take a while to get over the culture shock of recovery. Give your eyes a chance to adjust."

## Transvaluation of All Values

Jesus, it is said, turned the world upside down. In the Christian dispensation, weakness became valued as strength, slaves replaced their masters and ruled with what Nietzsche, in *The Genealogy of Morals*, called *ressentiment*.

Will became anti-will. An eon of decadence began. "One should not em-
bellish or dress up Christianity," wrote Nietzsche in *The Anti-Christ*:

> it has waged *a war to the death* against this *higher* type of man,
> it has excommunicated all the fundamental instincts of this
> type, it has distilled evil, the *Evil One*, out of these instincts —
> the strong human being as the type of reprehensibility, as the
> 'outcast.' Christianity has taken the side of everything weak,
> base, ill-constituted, it has made an ideal out of *opposition* to the
> preservative instincts of strong life; it has depraved the reason
> even of the intellectually strongest natures by teaching men to
> feel the supreme values of intellectuality as sinful, as mislead-
> ing, as *temptations*. The most deplorable example: the depraving
> of Pascal, who believed his reason had been depraved by origi-
> nal sin while it had only been depraved by his Christianity! [22]

Nietzsche defined Christianity as the "harmful vice" of "active sympathy for the ill-constituted and weak." [23] When looked at through the
inverting lenses of Christ crucified, the symptoms of man's weakness
became legitimated. The "Good News" of the New Testament was for
the poor in spirit. Whatever they could not absorb about themselves,
the suffering Christ of vicarious atonement would absorb for them. The
weak and afflicted gained an advocacy in the teachings of Jesus. Like
diseased sheep huddling together for warmth, Christians enacted what
Nietzsche called their "herd morality."

After Jesus turned the world upside-down, Peter, the "rock" upon
which Christ built his Church, became the cornerstone of the institu-
tionalization of the Christian inversion of values by asking the Romans
to crucify him upside-down. The universal Catholic Church was built
from meekness and martyrdom and spread like a disease. As it grew, as
it encompassed more and more of the world within its sickly embrace,
the agoraphobics living inside it felt less shut in. Soon the soul itself was
declared to be naturally Christian.

Nietzsche took off the inverting glasses, the God-glasses, of
Christianity and stared down the Christian inversion of reality until it turned right-side-up again. He called his philosophic *oeuvre* "the
transvaluation of all values," by which he meant the subverting of the

Christian inversion of truth, in order to return culture to the Greek values of robust health, strength, proportion, and power.

To step out of Judeo-Christianity, to step out of the Great Code as Nietzsche did, is to expose oneself to the dizzying uncertainty of an absolute, yet personally discreet, creative freedom. When perception is released from the inverting glasses to which it has so long been accustomed, the world at first seems upside-down and we, perhaps, feel crazy. Weakened by several thousand years of grace, our strength will seem clumsy, our reason, hyperbolic and deranged. After walking so long in the flock, we find it difficult to walk on our own two legs again.

Nietzsche recognized this condition and affirmed the strength latent in it when he called himself the philosopher of convalescence. He suffered from blinding migraine headaches, dizziness, nausea, days of vomiting, congenital (?) syphilis, and, later, cerebral paralysis. These enervations, in his view, were strength values of the will returning from the repression (inversion) occasioned by vicarious religion. Absorbed into his own soul-making efforts, they were the streams, which fed the river of his ascending will to power, his *amor fati*, his "yes" to life. Nietzsche's life and death, and the vicissitudes he encountered in between, were his own. He did not give himself up to vicarious religion. By remaining ever on the side of strength, even when suffering the distress of his own post-Christian body, Nietzsche penetrated out of the Christian inversion of values, the cross of Christ crucified. As he expressed this himself in the final sentence of his last book: "Have I been understood? — Dionysus versus the Crucified." [24]

Scales Off Eyes

When the glasses come off, when one leaves the perceptual field of the traumatic complex, there may be a feeling of guilt, illegitimacy — even criminality.

A middle-aged woman, who had been sexually molested by a psy-chotic relative before the age of five, suffered a variety of debilitating phobias, including agoraphobia. With the assistance of a small network of "helpful" friends, this woman was able to remain shut up inside her house for several decades. This "upside-down" world was her "normal" world. So long as she lived in the eye of her trauma, she was quite com-fortable and free of anxiety, at least at the conscious level.

But then the inverting glasses began to come off. Several close rela-tives and several of her friends died. No longer was she able to enlist others to shop or run errands for her. No longer did she have a "sup-port-system" to facilitate her agoraphobia and lend consensus reality to her mode of being, or not-being, in the world. Suddenly, the "real world" came into focus, although it seemed a topsy-turvy world at first.

The woman turned to psychotherapy for help. Despite an escalation in her level of anxiety, she was able to steal out of her house to attend her individual and group therapy sessions. I say "steal," because entering the world she had so long been isolated from felt at first like stealing. The patient had long been used to living subversively, in her house, under her rock. She was used to back-doors and back-roads and the ordinances of her phobias.

Sadly, this kind of pathetic scenario is all too common. Divided against their own basic needs and desires, many people eek out a bare existence, often in the very midst of the plenty that they have become too inhibited to enjoy. What pleasure is taken in life is taken against what appears to be the requirements of a too-brutal reality principle, that is, indirectly, pervertedly.

At first, the afflicted one may feel illegitimate, bastardly, disinherit-ed, and ashamed. Eventually, however, these feelings lose their acuteness, giving way to a sense of "squatter's rights." Simply by the act of surviv-ing, simply by the act of re-articulating the world through his fears and avoidances, the neurotic ontologizes his disinheritance. With this de-velopment knowledge dawns, a knowledge composed of crooked insights and kinky conclusions. Having survived his abandonment to a traumati-cally-inhibited life situation, the neurotic finds that he has worked out its epistemology, sunken though this may be. Illegitimacy becomes his legitimacy; virtue is made of pseudo-necessity. Sure-footedly, he walks through the back-alleys of the soul with the instinct of a Kafkaesque dung beetle and the street-smarts of an orphan in a Dickens novel.

During her treatment, the patient had the following dream:

> I have a job. I am a typist or secretary. The whole cast from my favorite soap opera are working at the same place, and they are stealing things from the business. The boss is not there right now, and my soap-opera friends are encouraging me to steal too. I'm ashamed to admit it, but in the dream I joined them in the stealing.

The boss who is away may be taken to be the patient's anxiety neurosis or trauma. The soap-opera stars, likewise, may be taken to be the house-gods of her usual agoraphobic universe. For decades the patient has lived inside her trauma, watching soap operas on television. But here, in this dream, the soap-opera stars and the dream-ego transgress the boundaries of the complex and the rule of the trauma-boss. The patient had recently begun to leave her house and to appropriate ground in the wider world — if only, at first, in order to attend her therapy sessions. In these sessions she remembered — quite spontaneously — some of the repressed scenes of her early childhood molestations. This was a significant development. No longer inhibited by what she refused to remember, she was now able to handle the "molestation" that everyday life involves. Following the working-through of the traumatic memories, she took even more freedom for herself. No longer was she living vicariously through the lives of soap-opera stars. On the contrary, with the help of the example and encouragement they brought in her dream (Jungian theory speaks of the psyche's prospective function), she began stealing each day a little more of the world forbidden to her by her old traumatic complexes, until gradually she entered the kingdom that comes like a thief in the night, the kingdom of "ordinary unhappiness."

## Repetition Compulsion or the Acuity of the Wound

When we see a patient who is "complexed" by an event in the present which appears to be transparent to an analogous traumatic event, we tend to draw a simple equation granting etiological significance to the past event. That the present situation is difficult, that the patient abused during childhood is wary of seduction or usury by a friend, spouse, or the therapist leads us to assume that the patient has been severely hurt or even damaged by the earlier calamity. How unfortunate, we think to ourselves, that the patient's perception of the present is so distorted by past impressions that he is inexorably drawn to re-enact his traumatic past.

But let us consider another way of conceptualizing these apparent re-enactments or compulsions to repeat, a gnostic way that is against the grain. The patient's actions and perceptions, for all their distortion, are nevertheless at the same time valid; his transferences subtly true. Though appearing to be galvanized by the abuse of the past, he is actually perceiving by means of what once happened *what is always happening* — not just to him at some other time and place, but generally in life to us all.

Archetypal themes have been described as that which never was but always is. The abusive, traumatic, or more broadly and positively speaking, numinous event of the past is less important for what it *was* — hence the debate in psychoanalysis over the reality of these events — than for its compensatory portrayal of what always is. The historical actuality of life's horrors notwithstanding, these overwhelming events serve as organs of perception for themes in life today as before, ever and always. Seduction, to take but one example, is a ubiquitous phenomenon. We are not only dislocated from our will and desire by childhood seductions, but by the ten-thousand things of our adult lives as well. Treatment of symptomatic suffering which confines itself to the actualities of the past may dislocate us from an awareness of what the symptoms are on about in the present. Could it be that the adult who was abused as a child is better prepared for the world as a result? Do the symptoms of suspiciousness and distrust, hypervigilence and paranoia, which we explain through reference to events of the past have a subtle validity for the present? Do we lose the immediate life value of these acuities by taking their *déjà vu* quality literally and trying to historically reconstruct the traumatic scene? Said a different way, do those who have not suffered a particular calamity, and whose eyes have not been opened by its transgression upon their fate — are they not more subtly seduced by the culture to which they all too easily adapt? Are the troubled actually more conscious than the untroubled? Have their eyes — vigilant and scanning — been opened to the darker vision that underpins real seeing?

### The Archetypes of the Traumatic Unconscious

The compensatory potential of what Jung has variously called the "archetype," "collective unconscious," "objective psyche," "numinosum" and "self" may sometimes widen the dissociations and exacerbate the difficulties it has been activated to bridge or heal. While at one juncture of life the inner activation of a particular motif may influence perception, cognition, and affective experience in such a way that we find ourselves to be more or less adapted to situations we have never encountered before, [25] at another juncture, the idealized expectations inspired by the motif may act as a jaundice in the eye. Perceiving short-comings in our life-situation rather than opportunities, we may be given over to a finicky sense of entitlement to more. Or, taking the dirty end of the same stick, we may fall prey to a forlorn sense of alienation and despair. [26] Provoked by these Gnostic resistances, the archetype may then re-assert its imperatives, now with a traumatic intensity. Hell-bent on realizing itself anew through our bodies and our world, it may come upon us with such violent force that we are put out of our bodies and worlds in the process. It is in this way that the rent in the culture, the rent in religion, and the rent in God become a rent in us each as well.

Talk about being between or rock and a hard place, or worse still, of being in such a place without such a metaphor! When the world in which we actually find ourselves is grossly discrepant with the archetype's

designs upon the world, when our familial, social, and cultural environ-
ments are not adequately adapted to the trajectory of "God's will" as this
enacts itself through our lives, [27] we may find ourselves subject to the negative numinosity of the nonrepresentable archetype (the so-called *Ding an
sich*) in noniconic form as overwhelming affectivity, free-floating anxiety,
nameless dread — the Trauma-God.

Mathematically figured these noniconic manifestations of the unconscious can be expressed in ultra-symbolic terms as the infinitudes x and y.
I say "ultra-symbolic" here (in contrast to analysts who speak of the "pre-
symbolic") because equations written with these figures have frequently
been shown to signify realities within the world, which physics, chemis-
try, and psychology, too, were only later to discover. As Jung, overcoming
the traumatic math-phobia of his childhood, notes in his memoirs, "the
properties of numbers are . . . simultaneously the properties of matter, for
which reason equations can anticipate its behavior." Substantiating this
claim with an example, Jung states further that "equations governing the
turbulence of heated gases existed long before the problems of such gases
had been precisely investigated." What is true of the math is true of myth
and symbol as well: ". . . we have long been in possession of mythologems
which express the dynamics of certain subliminal processes, though these
processes were only given names in very recent times." [28]

As suggestive as such occasional dove-tailings of spirit and matter may be, it is often the case, as deconstruction has argued, that our
equations and computations are discontinuous with the world they may
or may not model. Though "God ever arithmetizes," [29] the relationship
between His equations and our anxieties may be far from clear. God's
arithmetic can certainly be a trauma!

Is this why anxiety dreams so frequently draw upon the metaphor
of the mathematics exam? Even when we have been proficient at mathematics in actual life, we may dream that we are anxiously trying to solve
problems in this venerable subject. Do our traumas arithmetize, too?

$2x-y=a+b+$ . . . ??? The mathematics exam, which we recurrently
dream that we are failing (to say nothing of literal math anxiety), is indicative of the fact that the algebra of the archetypes and the geometry
of the spirit are always on a collision course with the crooked lines of life.

The Trinity is but one example. While as a theological dogma that conceives of God in three persons the notion of the Trinity may, like an isos-
celes triangle, perfectly inhere in the logic of its internal relations (the
square of the hypotenuse equalling the sum of the two sides), the dyna-
mism of such a symbolic notion in psyche and life, being a function of the
basic nonrepresentability of its archetypal essence, tends to express itself,
or rather, inflict itself upon us in an utterly disturbing manner. In this
connection we may be put in mind of Brother Klaus, the patron saint of
Switzerland, whose face, it is believed, was permanently disfigured by a
vision of the Trinity.[30]

Jung was right: "the gods have become diseases." Not only does "Zeus
no longer rule Olympus but rather the solar plexus,"[31] we now eschew as
panic attack and anxiety disorder what was once mediated for us, if only by
means of such propitiatory words as "God" and "Trinity," as the indwelling
power of a relentless, inaugurating spirit. Little wonder that we owe the
introduction of the term "anxiety" (*Angst*) to a theologian.[32]

Defending ourselves from the fact that the "pleroma," as Jung put it,
"is rent in us," we comfort ourselves with the anaesthetic of a platitude.
Recalling the words of Robert Browning — "a man's reach should exceed
his grasp, else what's a heaven for" — we forestall for a moment the recognition that the gap dividing our reach from our grasp is precisely what
can make life feel like hell. $2x-y=a+b+ \ldots ???$ — indeed!

It is the role of culture, as on a much smaller scale it is the role of
dreams, to span this gap with bridging symbols even as it is the mission
of each successive symbol of our cultural canon to *be* the squared hypotenuse in which both life and spirit tally. No symbol, however, can ever be
this for long. Always new forms are required to match the changes in the
tenor of the times. But as each of us heeds the imperative of the archetype (its inner constellation signalled by an anxiety dream about math),
each may find himself heartened by a sense of destiny or call.

The jaundiced eye sees all this rather differently. Cynically asserting
the impossibility of ever achieving adequate symbolic forms, it has ush-
ered in the so-called postmodern era in which our focus has changed from
the building of bridges to the demolishing or deconstructing of them.
But when the passionate living of life has been effaced by critical theory,

the Gods, enraged by our failure to observe them in new forms, become pitted once again against the titanic needs over which they had earlier prevailed. In our dreams and nightmares we are as modernist as ever.

It is characteristic of a time in which the culture no longer mediates the imperatives of the archetypal world that the sensible world becomes inundated by these imperatives in a confusing, traumatic, or insane manner. Collective symbols become personal symptoms, the Word a psychosomatic disorder. Said another way, without a sufficiently vital intermediary area of shared cultural forms, the green meerschaum pipe in René Magritte's painting, "This is not a pipe," ceases to be the work of art it so insistently claims to be, and becomes instead, like the paraphiliac's shoe which is not a shoe, the fallen receptacle of a fetishist's erotic intent! But the fact that a man may mistake a shoe for a woman or his wife for a hat is not only to be explained as a symptom of neurological disorder, as it was in the famous case of Dr. Oliver Sacks; such episodes of spilt algebra, sunken metaphoricity, and *psychopathia sexualis* are also indicative of the noetic malaise of contemporary culture. We live in a time in which everything is interchangeable with everything else, the random aim of a hand gun functioning in a grossly underdetermined manner as the profane equivalent or anti-type of the fingers in the Sistine Chapel. Bang, bang; bang, bang, bang. No longer subject to the "terrible initiative caress of God," [33] or, rather, so identified with it that we can no longer think in such terms, we now take pot shots at each other as if we were God, the algebraic mytheme of God touching Adam into life abortively miscarrying its incarnational imperative to become, like some Buffalo Bill defunct, the Washington-area Sniper.

Ave Maria, $2x-y=a+b+ \ldots$ ???, ave Maria. The angel that comes to Mary in our day is a terrible angel — angels and Mary having become defunct in our time, Gabriel some serial killer. Cribbing a theorem of Jung's, however, may hearten us as we struggle to find new ones: *Job's silence when faced with Yahweh's cruelty is already an annunciation of Christ.* [34] Playing this theorem forward, well might we yet ask with Yeats: and what rough beast, its hour come round at last, slouches towards New York, Washington, Bali, Moscow, and Baghdad to be born?

1. Sigmund Freud, *Beyond the Pleasure Principle*, trans. James Strachey (New York: W.W. Norton & Co., 1961), p. 30.

2. Ibid., pp. 32–33.

3. Ibid., p. 34.

4. Ibid.

5. Ibid., pp. 34–35.

6. Ibid., p. 20.

7. Ibid.

8. Ibid., p. 21.

9. Ibid., p. 26.

10. Friedrich Nietzsche, *Thus Spoke Zarathustra*, trans. R.J. Hollingdale (New York: Penguin Books, 1961), p. 69.

11. Freud, *Beyond the Pleasure Principle*, p. 26.

12. Ibid., p. 12.

13. Ibid., p. 21.

14. Ibid.

15. John Keats, *Selected Poems and Letters*, p. 288.

16. Freud, *Beyond the Pleasure Principle*, p. 21.

17. Ibid., p. 25.

18. Ibid., p. 26.

19. C.G. Jung, CW 9.1: 51–154.

20. Sigmund Freud, "Analysis Terminable and Interminable," CP 5: 345–46.

21. Freud, *Beyond the Pleasure Principle,* p. 35.

22. Friedrich Nietzsche, *Twilight of the Idols* and *The Anti-Christ*, trans. R.J. Hollingdale (Harmondsworth: Penguin Books, 1968), p. 117.

23. Ibid., p. 116.

24. Friedrich Nietzsche, *On the Genealogy of Morals* and *Ecce Homo*, trans. W. Kaufmann (New York: Vintage Books, 1967), p. 335.

25. One thinks, for example, of our innate ability to make use of significant people in our lives, such as therapists, as selfobjects.

26. Borrowing a term from Winnicott we could describe this as "negative use."

27. In Winnicott's view, the "good-enough mother" assists her child in its omnipotent creation of her by adapting herself to its wishes and needs during earliest infancy.

28. C.G. Jung, *Memories, Dreams, Reflections*, p. 311.

29. The adage originates with the nineteenth-century mathematician C.O. Jacobi.

30. C.G. Jung, CW 1: 478.

31. C.G. Jung, CW 13: 54.

32. Søren Kierkegaard

33. Thomas à Kempis, *De Imitatione Christi.*

34. Cf. Jung: "Faced with Yahweh's cruelty, Job is silent. This silence is the most beautiful and most noble answer that man can give to an all-powerful God. Job's silence is already an annunciation of Christ. In fact, God made himself man, became Christ, in order to redeem his injustice to Job." W. McGuire & R.F.C. Hull, eds., C.G. *Jung Speaking:Interviews and Encounters,* pp. 226–27.

chapter four


LIKE CURES LIKE

## Amor Fati

Overwhelming events, which cannot be incorporated into the life we have imagined for ourselves, cause the soul to bend back on itself, to commit "incest" with itself, and to revert to the heretical modes of the primary process. Like the festering action which removes the sliver from a wound, the traumatized imagination works and re-works its metaphors until the events which have "pierced" it can be viewed in a more adaptive fashion. Paradoxically, the challenge posed for the soul by the vicissitudes of nature and the shocks of life must be resolved by a movement *against* nature and *against* life. Alchemy knew this aspect of the work of soul-making as the *opus contra naturam*, the work against nature into culture which nature herself desires.

In his book, *An Outline of Psychoanalysis*, Freud defines the formation of the super-ego as a process based on the internalization of the external world: "A portion of the external world has, at least partially, been given up as an object and instead, by means of identification, taken into the ego — that is, has become an integral part of the internal world." [1] According to Freud, the ways in which the external world bumps, bruises, and overwhelms us gradually becomes introjected and, in the normal course of events, comes to discipline and rule the internal world. But when the external world has impinged upon the boundary of the body-self or upon the boundary of the ego severely enough to cause a shock or trauma, its internalization in the service of the reality principle obliterates the imaginal process of the soul's making.

The last thing that a punctured, leaky, hystericized soul needs is more "reality." Treatment aimed at adaptation to normative models or internalization of the reality principle merely adds insult to injury. To the traumatized soul the reality principle is a murdering parent, and this is something that cannot be cured by identifying with this aggressor any further.

And, yet, the marks of the real are inscribed upon us — both alienating trauma and personal fatality at once. The very traumas that threaten to obliterate us are also our most defining challenges. "Though he slay me, yet shall I trust him," exclaims the traumatized Job. (Job 1:4–5). Struggling in the cure to come to our own particular version of this awareness, we repeatedly find that our attempts to translate our symptoms into prose fail and our only recourse is to go on with them as poetry.

Nietzsche believed that if we are fool enough to affirm our fatality we will become wise. His notions of the "convalescent philosopher," "*amor fati,*" and "eternal recurrence" recognize the transformative value of embracing the symptoms that constitute our fate:

> My formula for greatness in a human being is *amor fati*: that one wants nothing other than it is, not in the future, not in the past, not in all eternity. Not merely to endure that which happens of necessity, still less to dissemble it — all idealism is untruthfulness in the face of necessity — but to *love* it . . . [2]

Our personal fatality is the ink-well out of which we write our personal mythology, our *amor fati,* our "yes" in the face of necessity. Unable to conform to normative models, the traumatized soul must invent its own until, as Keats wrote, ". . . branched thoughts, new grown with pleasant pain, instead of pines shall murmur in the wind." [3]

The pernicious thing about normative models and the notion of normal development is that they are essentially *static.* They are fixed on the Aristotelian notion of growth as an unfolding process or *entelechy* where the mature tree is from the beginning contained in the tiny kernel. But life has never enacted itself in such trauma-free laboratory conditions. In the laboratory, where processes enact themselves without having to contend with the force of other influences, they can follow in their father's footsteps. But outside the laboratory, life forms are constantly challenged, perturbed, decentered and traumatized by external reality in ways they cannot internalize. In order to contend with this murdering paternal stimuli impinging upon them, they must undergo evolutionary change, genetic drift, the creation of a personal mythology.

Therapy, when it does not respect the evolutionary character of fatality, risks placing its patients in laboratory conditions, aborting their soul-making process and then giving up on them as contaminated samples. If the earliest forms of life on this planet had enacted themselves in trauma-free laboratory conditions, the complexity of life forms populating our present world would not have emerged. We would have followed in the father's footsteps and remained, like him, a single-celled organism.

This brings us to Jung's notion of incest. In Jung's view, those portions of the libido that cannot move forward into life to form what Freud would call realistic "object-cathexis" can re-order themselves and cure themselves by regressing back into the maternal embrace of the collective unconscious. If the regressing libido is followed back to psychic layers "anterior to sexuality," the resultant "incest" will not be with the personal mother of the Oedipus complex, but with the Great Mother.

> The so-called Oedipus complex with its famous incest tendency changes at this level to a "Jonah-and-the-Whale" complex, which has any number of variants, for instance the witch who eats children, the wolf, the ogre, the dragon, and so on. Fear of incest turns into fear of being devoured by the mother. The regressing libido apparently desexualizes itself by retreating back step by step to the presexual stage of earliest infancy. Even there it does not make a halt, but in a manner of speaking continues right back to the intra-uterine, pre-natal condition and, leaving the sphere of personal psychology altogether, irrupts into the collective psyche where Jonah saw the "mysteries" (*représentations collectives*) in the whale's belly. The libido thus reaches a kind of inchoate condition in which, like Theseus and Peirithous on their journey to the underworld, it may easily stick fast. But it can also tear itself loose from the maternal embrace and return to the surface with new possibilities of life. [4]

When we cannot follow in the father's footsteps, when a trauma has erected a "Do Not Enter" sign above reality's door, we must regress to the mother's bed, dip our pens into the psychic gene pool of the collective unconscious, and return to the surface to write our personal mythology. As the fatality of the traumatized soul, the Oedipus complex is less a complex to be resolved than a psychology to be affirmed.

When development is thwarted mutation begins. Turned back upon itself by a trauma, forced to incestuously fertilize itself, the soul is on the cutting edge of evolutionary change. Viewed in this perspective, the individuation process of the traumatized soul is less the unfolding development of the *a priori* coding of what it was always meant to be, than it is a deviation or trans-mutation into something entirely new.

"You higher men," exclaims Nietzsche's Zarathustra, addressing those who should have realized that their lives are a fatality,

> do you suppose I have come to set right what you have set wrong? Or that I have come to you that suffer to bed you more comfortably? Or to you that are restless, have gone astray or climbed astray, to show you new and easier paths?
> No! No! Three times no! Ever more, ever better ones of your kind shall perish — for it shall be ever worse and harder for you. Thus alone — thus alone, man grows to the height where lightning strikes and breaks him: lofty enough for lightning. [5]

## When Two Or More Are Gathered Together

The traumatized soul, the soul that cannot make a difference between itself and the overwhelming event that it compulsively repeats, is today frequently treated in homogeneous support groups. When a patient becomes a member of a group of persons who have been traumatized by a similar event, he or she can begin to make distinctions *within* the event, which had previously proven so personally transcending. As each person tells the group what they can about how they were traumatized, each person's trauma gains specificity and particularity.

Jane, Cathy, Margaret, and Susan may all use the word "rape" to refer to the trauma they have suffered, but when they learn of the differences between each of their assaults they may begin to *experience* the *discrete* proportions of the events they had each been previously unable to relativize. Cathy's date-rape and Margaret's gang-rape, though both traumatizing assaults, display something of their particularity when compared with each other. When Susan relates how her attacker laughed and wore a mask and Margaret relates how her attacker attempted to strangle her with an electric cord, still more specificity is introduced. As they compare events, the compared events become experiences. Each woman gradually comes to realize that the creature who raped her is not an omnipotent, omniscient and omnipresent God, but in one case a two-hundred pound trucker with halitosis, in another an economics student from the local college, and in still another case a gang of drunken boys. Each woman must come to realize that the rapist that raped her is not a cosmic rapist and that every rape she reads about in the newspaper is not another of his exploits. In therapy it is crucial to compare details in order to expose the contingent features of a trauma, for if the patient is to make a difference between herself and her trauma she must begin to strip her attacker of the God-like proportions that galvanize her imagination.

Whenever two or more are gathered together in the name of a trauma, the events that had overwhelmed each will be exposed as relative and absorbed into soul. No matter how closely one trauma resembles another, and no matter how similar the terms are which we use to refer to them, two of a kind does not exist. There are as many Vietnams as there were men in action, and when the capacity of a veteran to imagine his life forward is dwarfed by events that have staggered his imagination, he must relativize this phenomenon by comparing it with the way war trauma has staggered the imaginations of other veterans.

Although, at first, we may not be able to distinguish between ourselves and an overwhelming event, we can take a first step toward this goal by making distinctions between instances of this inability. How do I differ from what I most resemble? How does my traumatic response differ from the traumatic response of others? How does the event that has overwhelmed me differ from similar events that have overwhelmed others? If we are made in the image and likeness of the trauma that has overwhelmed us, why are we still so different? Why does my traumatization take this particular form and not another?

Misery loves company. As each member of the support group hears the stories told by the other members, each is relieved of the compulsion to create a relativizing context for their trauma by repeating it themselves. While over time an individual may be able to manufacture a sufficient number of variations on her trauma's theme to relativize its core anxieties, the stories of other people who have be overwhelmed in a similar way can immediately provide the context through which healing comes. If Jane can have access to the stories of Cathy, Margaret and Susan, her compulsion to generalize the eliciting stimulus of her trauma to other situations in life may be less necessary and less strong. As they tell her what they remember, she may have less need to repeat what she cannot remember and vice versa. The various members of the group, simply by being other, provide a scale of values, a variety of differences. Margaret's gang rape and Susan's near strangulation were the more explicitly violent assaults, but Jane's rape by a man she knew and loved was more violating of her sense of trust in even familiar and apparently gentle men. As each woman shares the gruesome details of her own rape, rape becomes particularized in such a way that each woman can differentiate herself from it. Though the proportions of the event had transcended each group member's previous experience and, hence, each member's previous capacity to make experiences, it may still be seen in proportion when placed in a context of comparable events. By dividing the totalized trauma amongst themselves, its victims can strip it of its immeasurable quality, conquer and assimilate it.

Of course, when two or more are gathered together there is the danger that the group will degenerate into a mere denomination of vicarious religion. If the group's leader or therapist extracts generalities from the group members' accounts of their traumatization, the cosmic sense of the eliciting stimulus will be heightened and preserved. The support group approach goes off the track when events that have yet to be experienced and absorbed are pooled together and given a huge name that installs them quite beyond the reach of precise specification and experience — "post-traumatic stress disorder," "rape adjustment disorder," "domestic abuse." The group members learn the impersonal facts about the trauma they are said to suffer in common. As if reciting a liturgy, the therapist recites statistics from a sociology text. The group is told that a woman is being raped every nine minutes. But whenever "rape," "domestic violence," "Vietnam," or "Alcoholism" are spoken of in the abstract, worship is going on.

William Blake, in his critique of organized religion, was very clear on this point. After the "ancient Poets animated all sensible objects with Gods or Geniuses," he writes,

> [a] system was formed, which some took advantage of, &
> enslav'd the vulgar by attempting to realize or abstract the

mental deities from their objects: thus began Priesthood;
Choosing forms of worship from poetic tales.[6]

When therapy abstracts "mental deities" or impersonal categories from
the minute particularity of events, it loses its poetic basis and substitutes
a priestly one. The individual character of the patients' individual stories gets lost as the church fathers of psychology and sociology establish
their approved gospel canon of research findings. The cure that comes
through particularizing events into experiences, the cure that comes
through soul-making, becomes a heresy.

## The Eucharist of Sexual Assault

The dreamer is a thirty-year-old career woman, wife, and mother.
Although she was raised Roman Catholic, she converted to Protestantism
while a student at university and was later ordained as a Minister. The
dreams reported here were dreamt at a time when the dreamer was working through issues related to the oral rape she had suffered as a twelve-
year-old child. For years this trauma had unconsciously played a shaping
role in the dreamer's life. With the birth of her first child, however, a direct confrontation with the repressed feelings associated with the trauma
was triggered. The innocence of her newborn daughter reminded her of
the manner in which her innocence had been lost. Out of this crisis she
became involved with a local rape crisis center. Working with her trauma
and with the challenges this posed for her faith, she gradually began to
integrate her understanding of God with her experience of trauma, writing liturgies and prayers for those who have been violated.

About two years after she became a volunteer in the rape crisis center, she had the following dream:

> I am at a large hospital where hundreds of women who have
> been raped are gathered together. I go to one doctor upstairs.
> There is another large room downstairs filled with women

who are being treated by another doctor. This doctor, I hear, is suctioning all of the sperm out of the raped women. It sounds comforting to me. Though I am actually upstairs, I feel as though I am part of the group; we have all been raped. But then I have a flashback to my own experience and I feel scared and alone.

This dream images the breakdown of the dreamer's progressive defenses. Although she feels at one with the hundreds of rape victims on the first floor of the hospital, she is, in fact, on the second floor, looking on from above, her own trauma-laden affect isolated until it breaks through in a flashback to her own rape. Evidently, the defensive posture of ministering to herself — and then later, as a professional clergy-person, of ministering to others — has set her apart from the sisterhood of women whose soul-making activities, together in a homogeneous support group, helps them to absorb their traumas even as it helps them to draw off the semen which was forced into them. In her life, the dreamer is usually up in a pulpit preaching to a congregation or up on a podium delivering a lecture on sexual violence. Seldom has she had the opportunity to simply be a "sister" among "sisters," a sufferer sharing as an equal with those who have suffered in similar ways. Rather, on the second floor of the hospital, up in the pulpit, she is still in thrall to the assault of her childhood. The *logos spermatikos*, the spermy word of the divine to whose ministry she has been ordained, still bears the traumatic stamp of the oral rape she suffered as a girl. While delivering sermons and offering prayers that are helpful to others, the Trauma-God continues to rape her in her pastoral countertransference.

The movement of the dream as a whole seems to be away from the spirituality of the dream-ego's rape-trauma toward the soulful sorority of it. Although she cannot yet appreciate it, it is in the flashback to her own rape scene — with all its attendant feelings of terror and isolation — that she is more than superficially at one with the other women. It is the progressive defense against these feelings, the adoption of a ministering or missionary stance, that divides her from her sisters.

The next dream (from the same night) explores more fully the tangled nexus of trauma, progressive defense, and religion.

I arrive at a church to hear Marie Fortune[7] speak. As I come in I see Marie dressed in a cool grey alb. I have a good feeling about seeing her again.

The talk about sexual assault and abuse begins. An older man re-enacts how he began to sexually abuse his five-year-old daughter. It is dark and the audience is milling around. We are outside. I see the man find the little girl, who is lying on the table, nude. He begins stroking her leg, then her genitals. This is how it began.

Then we are gathered in an L-shaped room like the downstairs of an old house. I am part of the audience. I want to say something noteworthy. I raise my hand and talk about how the abuse became an erotic obsession, like a religion. If anything I have sympathy for the man, not the girl, in spite of what I heard: that he stuck something through her belly button and inflated her uterus so that the girl's periods began. I think that the girl was disabled after that — some kind of misfit.

When I try to make my intelligent remark, I find that I have a big wad of gum in my mouth so that I can't get my words out. Then I return [to myself]. The speaker asks me whether I am a nurse. I proudly say that I am a minister.

The talk concludes and I volunteer to drive Marie to the airport since I am going past it to where my mother lives and is looking after my son. We can't find Marie's alb and we look all over the church for it. We still can't find it. There is some kind of dinner meeting going on.

Religion is concerned with those aspects of existence that transcend, overwhelm, and traumatize us. If we lived in a world where events did not exceed our capacity to come to terms with them immediately and directly, we would have no impulse toward religion. Christianity institutionalized an abstract, generalized relationship to trauma. So abstract and general is the Church's relationship to trauma, in fact, that we soon forget that it is based in trauma and see only the actions of a loving Father, even when that Father is crucifying his only begotten Son.

But sometimes our individual traumas do not get fully absorbed into the Church's abstract containers. Indeed, sometimes individual traumatic events style our relationship to religion itself, rendering it idiosyncratic and personal. Though we all repeat the liturgy in unison, we may each take up the notion of a transcendent God in terms of the individually specific ways in which we have been transcended and traumatized in our lives. For the minister whose dreams we are examining, the traumatic model through which she takes up the notion of a transcendent God was the sexual assault she suffered at the age of twelve. The man who assaulted her, the man who dominated her and forced her to perform fellatio on him, transcended her. Immediately after the attack her life became ritualistic and religious. Shadows became charged with menace, the numinosity of the traumatized. She lived constantly with the awareness that she could again be overwhelmed by transcending spirit, even if that transcending spirit were only the transcending will of another attacker. [8]

In the second dream we see that despite the eighteen years that have elapsed since her rape (or, rather, as a result of them), religion is still unconsciously conceptualized in terms of sexual assault. Standing in for the communion table, where matter was transubstantiated into spirit in the days of her Roman Catholic innocence, is the communion table of child sexual abuse, where matter is turned into spirit in a fashion closer to her own actual experience. Despite the fact that the man at this altar had "stuck something through [the girl's] belly button and inflated her uterus so that [her] periods began," despite the fact that he aroused the girl's libido before she is old enough to handle it (according to Freud's early and Ferenczi's later seduction theory), the dream-ego finds that her sympathy is with him, the abuser. Wanting to say something "noteworthy" she explains that the man's abusive behavior "became an erotic obsession, like a religion." This is an important aspect of the dream. It reflects the Protestantism into which her sexual assault had initiated her.

But the dream takes a turn in another direction. When she tries to make her intelligent remark she finds that her mouth is filled with a big, sticky wad of gum — a reference to her oral rape (her association). The mouthful of gum in the second dream, like the flashback to the rape scene in the first dream, points to the same thing: the breakdown of her progressive defenses and of her unwitting identification with the aggressor. To the extent that the dreamer's usual priestly function is taken over by the high-priest Marie Fortune, to the extent that she finds herself in the congregation amongst the sisterhood of the afflicted, she is tongue-tied by the unassimilated substance of her trauma.

At the end of the dream, Marie Fortune's alb (clergy gown) is mislaid and cannot be found. Although the searching dream-ego is still committed to her trauma in its religious dress, the dream as a whole seems to be dislocating it from the priestly garment in which it has been robed.

With the loss of the Protestant alb, the dreamer's movement from Roman Catholicism to Protestantism is taken a step further. Protestantism was a protest against priesthood. In Protestantism the gulf between the priest and the laity was narrowed. Each man became his own priest, the celebrant of the mystery of his own trauma, even as our dreamer became a minister herself. Protestantism reclaimed trauma from the priestly exclusivity of Catholicism and allowed a variety of denominational sensitivities and responses. But with the loss of the alb of Protestantism, an even further step is taken. The eucharist of vicarious priesthood de-transubstantiates itself right back into the gummy mouthful of her own personal trauma. Absorbing this gummy mouthful, without the slippery coating of vicarious religion, is what the mystery of "ordinary unhappiness" is all about.

Judge Schreber's Trauma

Daniel Paul Schreber (b. 1842), the author of the memoirs upon which Freud based his influential paper "Psycho-Analytic Notes Upon an Auto-biographical Account of a Case of Paranoia (*Dementia Paranoides*)," was well acquainted with the Trauma-God.

> From the first beginnings of my contact with God up to the present day my body has continuously been the object of divine miracles . . . Hardly a single limb or organ in my body escaped being temporarily damaged by miracles, nor a single muscle being pulled by miracles . . . Even now the miracles which

I experience hourly are still of a nature to frighten every other human being to death. [9]

Freud's analysis of the case stresses Schreber's clearly homosexual attitude toward "God," and interprets Schreber's delusions of persecution as a backlash of his having projected his latent homosexual tendencies outside himself. In place of the proposition "I (a man) *love him* (a man)," the paranoiac, according to Freud, substitutes the proposition "I do not *love* him — I *hate* him." This defensive deployment of projection and reaction formation is then bolstered by the idea, "I do not *love* him — I *hate* him, because HE PERSECUTES ME." [10]

> An internal perception is suppressed, and, instead, its content, after undergoing a certain degree of distortion, enters consciousness in the form of an external perception. In delusions of persecution the distortion consists in a transformation of affect; what should have been felt internally as love is perceived externally as hate. [11]

Freud's analysis, being based solely on Schreber's memoir, is incomplete in that the influence of the physical and emotional abuse which the Judge suffered as a boy is not considered. But, as Niederland has shown, [12] Schreber's father, an eminent physician and writer on education, held rather sadistic views about child discipline. In several books published on the subject, Schreber senior describes a variety of torturous methods for correcting children. For instance, if a child does not hold his head up straight, the elder Schreber recommended tying the child's hair to its underwear with cords. Likewise, children who do not sit straight in their chairs could be harnessed in a contraption that would press an iron bar into their collarbones should they slouch. To toughen up a child, Schreber's father recommended that infants from the age of three months be washed in cold water.

Niederland's re-examination of the Schreber case suggests that objective correlatives for many of Schreber's persecutory delusions can be found in the sadistic child-rearing prescriptions practised by his father. The traumatizing God of Judge Schreber's memoirs, Niederland's analysis suggests, is none other than the God of his own tortured child-hood, his abusive father. This view of Schreber's delusions, Niederland reminds us, is in keeping with Freud's latter idea that in hallucinations "something that has been experienced in infancy and then forgotten re-emerges . . ." [13]

Niederland's re-examination of the Schreber case necessitates a re-examination of the relationship Freud drew between paranoia and repressed homosexuality. When persecutory delusions are derived from traumas and *not* from projected homosexuality, what are we to make of the "homosexual" features that may nevertheless accompany them? Or better put: if Schreber's paranoia was at bottom a result of the traumatic abuse he suffered as a child, what is the relationship between paranoia, homosexuality and trauma?

Paranoid delusions with a homosexual coloration point to the failure of the *homoerotic imagination* to relativize the overwhelming events tyran-nizing over the traumatized soul in a God-like fashion. It is not that paranoia is a projection of the subject's ego-dystonic homosexuality, as Freud argued (though, of course, such projections can occur). Paranoid delusions of homosexual attack can also be symptomatic of a soul that is afraid of anything metaphorically or "homoerotically" akin to the origi-nal traumatic event. If a trauma has been especially severe, the soul may at first behave as if it were allergic to the cure that comes through like-ness. Initially, it may tend to flee from similar events as if they were the overwhelming event. Scanning the environment for signs of the event which had injured it, the soul cannot see the curative forest of resem-bling events for the immense tree that it is determined not to tangle with ever again. Each likeness that is mistaken for the original trauma, each metaphor that is taken literally, becomes, like the persecutory God of Schreber's delusions, a homosexual attacker. The therapeutic task at this point is to treat the homophobic literalism (the fear of likeness) so that the homoerotic imagination, which will ultimately heal the trauma, can be utilized once more.

## Parricide or the Making of Water

The move out of vicarious religion, the move out of the cult of the reified trauma, can be attended by homoerotic or homosexual effects. In *Totem and Taboo,* Freud associates a homosexual clubbing together of the primordial brothers with the dispatch of their tyrant father.

> Though the brothers had banded together in order to overcome their father, they were all one another's rivals in regard to the women. Each of them would have wished, like his father, to have all the women to himself. The new organization would have collapsed in a struggle of all against all, for none of them was of such over-mastering strength as to be able to take on his father's part with success. Thus the brothers had no alternative, if they were to live together, but — not, perhaps, until they had passed through many dangerous crises — to institute the law against incest, by which they all alike renounced the women whom they desired and who had been their chief motive for despatching their father. In this way they rescued the organization which had made them strong — and which may have been based on homosexual feelings and acts, originating perhaps during the period of their expulsion from the horde.[14]

When the trauma we have learned to call "father" or "God" is stripped of its authority, we become aware of the potency we have collectively projected, as well as of the inferiority and inadequacy that these projections had protected us from. Consciousness becomes a double-consciousness, an ambivalence of potency and impotence, power and vulnerability. At this point a homosexual coloration can appear, as we try to sort our individual creative potential out from that of our brothers.

A man who was just in the process of breaking out of the cult of projected creativity to become more fully the creator of his own life dreamt that he stood at a urinal in a men's washroom. Around him, crowding him on all sides at nearby urinals, other men were similarly engaged. The dreamer felt uncomfortable at the lack of privacy in this strange men's room and shy at the comparative smallness of his penis. As he tried to push his way out of the crowded washroom, the huge penises of the other men touched him. He felt disgusted, inadequate, intruded upon, inferior, and afraid.

One's own discreet creative power is hard to size up, hard to measure. In a public washroom we stand on our own two feet and make our own living water. There are no vicarious supports or religious containers — except, perhaps, that infernal scripture of graffiti that is written above the urinal.

Let us imagine Freud, Adler, and Jung bumping into each other in some vulgar little washroom after a meeting at a psychoanalytic congress. One can imagine Freud, the atheist, a man self-consciously aware of his own creative power, stoically attempting to master what he once called in a letter to Jung an "unruly homosexual feeling" while peaking over at his colleagues to ascertain whether or not they are circumcised to his — their psychoanalytic father's — will. Adler, meanwhile, we can imagine, trying to relax a shy bladder while dreaming up his theory of organ inferiority and overcompensation. (Adler, by the way, later converted from his Jewish faith to protestant Christianity.) Standing between them is Jung (we imagine) pissing uninhibitedly, loud and long, the devotee and favorite of the God who shat upon the Basel cathedral in his childhood fantasy. [15]

Freud struggled with a greater burden of homosexual feelings than Jung did because he saw religion as an illusion whereas Jung did not. When relationship matters were addressed in their letters, Jung confessed to Freud that he had an ambivalent "'religious' crush" [16] on him, the traumatic model of which was the sexual abuse he suffered as a child or youth at the hands of a man he had idolized. [17] Unable to face the intimacy of their creative equality with all its homoerotic tensions, Jung briefly projected his creativity into the worship of Freud. He protected himself from equality by styling himself as Freud's son, only to later disparage the inequality and berate Freud as a tyrant. Of course, Freud's overly literal conception of homoerotic feelings didn't help the situation. Freud shrank away from an equal relationship into materialistic propitiations of the homoerotic feelings no less than Jung shrank from them into spiritualized avoidances.

As great as the accomplishments of Freud and Jung have been as the founders of rival viewpoints, they fell far short of the possibilities available to them had they been able to cooperate. Constellated in the relationship between them was the psychic energy pent-up for millennia in the supernatural containers of their Hebrew and Christian culture. In the early years of this century, psychoanalysis was pregnant with the total renewal of culture. But the pregnancy was aborted. Unable to work through their homoerotic transferences, Freud and Jung parted ways.

A man, whose decision to enter analysis reflected a movement out of vicarious religion and into the active making of his own psychology, dreamt that he was in his parents' backyard. The huge tree that had dominated the yard had been cut down, reduced to a stump. Throughout the yard, the roots of the felled tree sent up shoots by the hundreds. The shoots, it seemed, were penises.

This dream, like the men's washroom dream, images the multiplication of penises that accompanies the renunciation of vicarious religion and the restoration of creative power to man. The two dreams reflect a psychology that has begun to penetrate out of the covenant of circumcision. Penetrating out of the covenant of circumcision means penetrating out of the religious assurances that God will make of us a great nation. It means standing at one's own little urinal, no longer allowing the conjectures of Abraham's penis to reach beyond the discrete possibilities of one's own. It means the killing and breaking free of the totem and the taboo.

The female side of all this was termed "penis envy" by Freud. The concept of penis envy is a reductive and materialistic recognition of the struggle women have had assessing their potency in a male-dominated world. If it has been hard for men to stand at the urinal of their own creative destiny, it has been harder still for women. Fortunately, women have more and more become able to release themselves from their so-called penis envy and to assume responsibility for their own creativity. No longer do they conceive of themselves as the concubines of the circumcised. Following in the footsteps of their female peers, men, too, are beginning to penetrate out of their envy of the aggrandized phallus, which circumcision (i.e., the covenantal relationship with the vicarious phallus of a creator-God) has locked them into.

## Archetypal Psychology

James Hillman's move from the noumenal archetype to the archetypal or phenomenal image [18] provides a Jungian analogue to Freud's clinical mythology. The noumenal archetype, which has dominated Jungian thought like the tyrant father of Freud's *Totem and Taboo*, has led at times to ham-handed interpretations. In Hillman's writings, however, the images have banded together as brothers, killed the abstract archetype and eaten it. Like the father in the belly of his sons, "the archetype," writes Hillman, "is wholly immanent to its image." [19] The incest taboo comes into play with the same move that affirms the totem substitute: just as the brothers, according to Freud, renounced their desire to take possession of all the women — an act that would imprison the anima once more in a father's testicles — the archetypal school makes monotheism taboo. No single perspective, no one brother, may dominate the psyche, hording for itself the multiple possibilities of imagination and making.

## Into Her Own Hands

Feeling deeply betrayed by her husband, who seemed to regress to his unlived adolescence soon after their marriage, she dreamt that she was in a barren desert with her husband and father. The two men were naked. On the side of the van they had driven to the desert in her husband loaded beef carcasses into the vehicle, while, on the other side, her father squatted as if to defecate, but instead of the expected bowel movement his genitals fell off. Passively, the dream-ego looked on as if she had little to do with the whole transaction.

Marriage, betrayal, husband, father, castration and animal carcasses — absent in their presence and present in their absence, how do these construct and deconstruct each other?

Traditionally, marriage is a covenant, not only between a husband and a wife, but between the father of the bride and his son-in-law. In modern marriages the ceremonial practice still survives of the bride's father giving his daughter away. The two walk down the aisle together because the daughter is still considered to be the property of the father. But for the woman who dreamt this dream something had gone wrong with the marriage she had been given into and she felt betrayed.

In an earlier section mention was made of the ancient practice of swearing oaths upon the testicles. When Abraham wanted his servant to take an oath he said to him, "put thy hand under my thigh" (Gen. 24:2). Reversing this logic, castration reflects the breaking of a covenant, the betrayal of a trust. False testimonies break the promise of the testicles; covenants are broken in the groin.

The beef carcasses in the dream can also be referred to biblical notions of covenant. After a vision in which Yahweh proclaimed to Abraham his covenant with the Hebrew people assuring them a great future (Gen. 15:1), Abraham sacrificed an animal to Him as an act of faith. That night in his dream, Abraham saw "a smoking fire pot and a flaming torch" move between the pieces of the sacrificed animal. This dream of the ceremony of the covenant became a basic ritual in all contracts between men in ancient times. Contractual agreements were sealed by sacrificing an animal and walking between the halves of its carcass. With this ritual the parties to the contract demonstrated to one another that they would no more break their covenant with one another than be cut in half like a sacrificed animal.[20]

In the dream the husband takes the sacrifice while the father simply squats there like an emasculated shit. The feeling level of the dream seems to be saying: "Daddy, why didn't you save me from my husband? Why did you give me away without the promise and assurance of a good future? Daddy, you betrayed me by being taken in the bride-price deal; the imperfect covenant you made has caused me much, much pain."

On another level, however, the felt absences of the dream constellate presence. The dreamer's marriage, or rather, its termination, is the sacrifice that takes her out of the father's genitals. By means of a series of separations and then finally a divorce, she broke out of the testicular prison of her patriarchal legacy. Buying herself a diamond ring, she handed herself over into her own hands. Now, paradoxically, marriage as an individual relationship is possible. And in line with this, the personal friendship she maintained with her ex-husband is the new ground of a new culture. When the veil of marriage comes off the woman's face, and the testicles come off the old father, the two fundamental taboos of totemism are left behind: the prohibition against individual relationships between men and women and the prohibition against breaking out of the super-ego structures of an extinct culture.

## Lesbian Grounding

A middle-aged woman artist, who was just becoming aware of her tendency to project her creative power onto men ( accepting them as sexual partners or rejecting them accordingly), had the following dream:

> I am making love to an unknown woman. Our bodies form a perfect circle. Two vague, unknown men watch us. Apparently we are going to make love to them after we finish. The room we are in has only two walls (forming together a single corner). Behind the wall a vague, unknown woman is walking. We do not have sex with the men.

The lesbian love-making and the unacted prospect of making love to the men are precisions of the same image. The dream-ego makes love to her own sex precisely by not getting around to having sex with the men who watch nearby, and vice versa. The dreamer's heteroerotic tendency to project her creativity onto men in sexual relationships has become contained in lesbian embraces. The women perform cunnilingus on each other, their bodies forming a perfect circle. The dreamer's creativity is contained in its own feminine orbits. Although men are near and desirable, the dream-ego does not vicariously assign her creative power to them.

The room has two walls that form a single corner. Behind the wall walks a vague, unknown woman. Is this the old feminine tendency?

Is this the woman who would project her creative power onto men, making love to them without adequate lesbian grounding? Or is this the feminine creative principle returning from repression? I suppose it all depends on whether the dreamer can sustain her homoerotic stance or not.

A traumatic model for the forfeiture of feminine creative power to men is the primal scene. According to Freud, a child's first impressions of sexuality give rise to a "sadistic conception of coitus." [21] The child sees its father on top of its mother; it hears the moans and cries of coitus and believes that the father is beating the mother. When the child discovers that its mother lacks a penis while the father possesses one, the fantasy is formed that the father castrated her. If the child is a girl, she may believe that her father castrated her as well. If this happens, the girl will tend to resent her mother for not protecting her and will form an affectionate tie to the father whom she unconsciously fears could hurt her again.

In the artist's dream, the traumatic logic of the primal scene is being absorbed into soul. Although, at first, the women may possibly be licking each other's vaginas as if they were licking a castration wound, they are also mirroring each other, providing each other the homoerotic field of comparison necessary to bring into consciousness a wholly feminine conception of their creative power. If the dreamer is able to resist emasculating herself with the old mythology, if she is able to resist enlisting a man to be the carrier of her creative power, the lesbian cunnilingus will perhaps obtain this emancipating meaning.

### Homeopathic Imagination

The imagination tends to operate in terms of resemblances, likenesses, sames. One story leads to another story leads to another. We perceive things *homeopathically,* sometimes even *homoerotically,* in terms of brotherhoods and sisterhoods. We individuate objects and events into unique shapes by noticing how they differ from what they most resemble.

This homeopathic style of imagination, this attraction of like for like, is as natural as our own sensations. The smell of today's roses calls into play the absent roses, the roses of yesterday. The nose constructs their smell by an act of deconstruction. I smell my sensations by comparing them with my repressed sensations, the subtext, the latent homoerotic brotherhood of resembling sensations in memory. I smell the nuanced difference of these sames. But this natural bent of the mind, this play of resonance and resemblance, can be short-circuited by trauma.

An overwhelming event, an event for which we cannot find a field of comparison (and, therefore, cannot fully experience and absorb), is traumatic. A trauma is anything we cannot talk about in a Platonic dialogue. It is whatever we have a dogmatic relationship with or consider too sacred to blaspheme. It is whatever we cannot entertain as a fiction because we have turned it into a religion.

Trauma polarizes consciousness into opposites — black and white, male and female, pleasure and unpleasure, guilty or not-guilty. Heterogeneous imagination, the imaginational mode of the antithetical and opposite, has its source in trauma. An overwhelming event, an event which cannot be contained for lack of analogies, traumatizes and polarizes the mind. Something frightens or hurts us. We flee from it, if only by counter-phobically and seductively giving ourselves over to it. As matters escalate and greater and greater tensions develop between the opposites, the trauma repeats itself. Because of its heterosexual effects on the imagination, traumata are able to reproduce themselves in the mind.

To break out of the heterogeneous trauma cycle we need to enter the homeopathic mind. Like cures like. Our traumas can be healed by conversations and dialogues. Homogeneous support groups — groups for alcoholics, battered wives, incest survivors and sex offenders, etc. — can be medicinal. We can only turn an overwhelming event into an absorbable experience by comparing it with other resembling events. Together we can compare notes and read the larger story in terms of which we can locate ourselves uniquely, particularly, discretely.

## Trauma Anonymous

If whatever we do once is a trauma (for lack of a field of comparison), whatever we do twice is a ritual, a religion. Twice, three times, four, five — all numbers greater than one are an attempt to incorporate the first time, the number one.

The first cut is the deepest. One is always the biggest number. Jung even said that it is a fictive ideal and that the first real number is two. [22]

The variegated imaginal field, the ten-thousand things of the soul, the petit observances and obsessive compulsions of our day to day routines multiply and multiply again as if trying to engulf and incorporate the original fiat, the number one, the first time.

Mathematically speaking, the soul-making process is limitless. One event requires a second to give it a context as an experience. The second event then requires a third, the third a forth, and so on *ad infinitum*. All arithmetic is the festering exegesis of the unfathomable number, the number one.

The alcoholic, according to the popular adage, begins with his first drink; however, it would take a master of a not yet invented psychoanalytic calculus to measure the acceleration from that first drink to the second and to the last. Perhaps addiction is paradoxically an attempt to experience rather than an attempt to escape experience. Perhaps what locks the addict into the addiction is that in his repetitive bouts of substance abuse he is trying to *experience* his original "anti-experience" with the drug. From this perspective, each successive black-out is an attempt to remember and experience the first black-out. It is an obsession with the missing time, the forgotten hours, the spirit of absence, that drives the addict. He gets high not in order to lose himself in a fresh state of oblivion but, rather, to re-enter the original oblivion in the hope that he might find himself, the hours of himself that he has lost. It is not only that the chemicals addict physiologically. By depressing the nervous system and diminishing consciousness, the alcohol renders the cyclical process by which consciousness is made a game without end. The alcoholic's downward spiral is also an infinite regress.

By means of his second full bottle he searches for his first empty. But when he returns to his origins he does not see them as if for the first time. No sooner has he absorbed the substance of his trauma than he passes out again.

## Reading and Writing

Reading can be traumatic. It may take years for a student to take in what he reads. The material is at first too overwhelming. Hegel — what? Melville — what? Marx, Freud and Jung — what?

In essays and assignments the student repeats the trauma of his reading, paragraph after paragraph, page by page. If he is especially disturbed he may even find himself consulting the experts and reading study guides as if trying to develop in retrospect the pedantic anxiety or pedantic crust, whose lack occasioned his trauma in the first place. Turning to these secondary texts, the student attempts to assimilate the traumatic text. This, as we know, can go on for many years. In fatal cases, the student may even go on to become a professor. Spreading out the trauma of his reading, he may then, year after year, impose overwhelmingly large reading lists upon his freshmen classes.

Little wonder that our bookshelves burgeon so! Little wonder that we are inundated with more and more titles that we feel we "really should read." The comprehension that is so desperately needed proceeds by indirection. Sober understanding only very gradually dawns when enough of the field of comparison has been read.

But long before this has happened, many a traumatized reader finds that he has become, in his turn, a traumatized and traumatizing writer! Pelted by a veritable cascade of inscrutable texts, the reader is compelled to turn out texts of his own. Just a line from someone else's book is enough sometimes to inspire a book of one's own. Reader beware: to underline a sentence is to risk being taken under by it as Ahab was by his own harpoon line!

## Shit Happens

Once we imagined ourselves to be created by God, in His image, after His likeness. Now we grant to events, especially traumatic events, the same creative and destructive power as we once attributed to this supreme metaphor. But what, we must ask ourselves, does this imply about our sense of metaphor? And what are the consequences of this for our experience of events?

While it appeared, at first, that the death of God had freed the imagination to invent new metaphors, it is now becoming only too clear that the proliferation of supplanting images has merely infected the imagination of modernity with the same fatal malaise that claimed our faith in God. Though metaphor is currently in vogue, the subject of numerous dissertations, it has become, through our secularized and secularizing fascination with it, decadent and ineffectual, cut off from life. Worse still its death is near, as Deconstruction, hastening that death by performing early autopsies, exists to declare. No longer can tropes, such as Yeats's "blood-dimmed tide," forestall the "anarchy that is loosed upon the world," the senseless violence of abjected events.

Today, it is no longer monsters of the deep such as Behemoth and Leviathan which present images of the dark side of God; events do, plain, literal, contingent, events. Nor do we any longer cover our mouths, like Job, lest our quarrels and complaints seem impious to our Maker. On the contrary, in consulting rooms, courts of law, and television talk shows we cry out against our abusive parents, perverted uncles, course-mouthed colleagues, and sex-crazed employers as against the tyranny of unjust gods. Their wickedness — not the Devil's or God's — is the omnipotent force, which has shaped our lives. Like the Devil and God, the lingering effects of their misuse of us, repressed from awareness but recalled in visions called flashbacks, is, or so we have come to believe, the invisible power that works in mysterious ways.

Of course, we do propitiate *overwhelming* events as if they were God. The abused child does see his or her abuser as a tyrannical divinity even as pious believers unwittingly image God on the model of whatever has transcended them in their actual lives. These facts, however, must be balanced against others. For it is not merely overwhelming events of forensically verifiable abuse and torture that dwarf the imagination with their transcending power. Today, partly as a consequence of our mechanical philosophy's fixation on causality and partly as a consequence of what Jung called our malaise of "impoverished symbolism," [23] any event, even one that has *not* happened to us, but which we and our therapy culture merely believes must have happened, can be experienced in the same religio-traumatic way. Adapting the words of the Delphic oracle to our present purposes, it seems apt to say: Invoked or not invoked, the Trauma-God will be here.

It is not just that zealous therapists have abused patients by attributing their ills to trauma and abuse even when these have never happened. Adding well-meaning therapists to a list of perpetrators that has always included our well-meaning, if imperfect, parents is an ironic twist, but hardly a change in paradigm. In reckoning their interventions to have had ruinous consequences we are still viewing events in the same fashion.

We must think critically about our contemporary God-terms, "Abuse" and "Trauma," and about the ways these have been turned into buzz words of the therapy cult. This is not in any way to deny the actuality of trauma and abuse. There is no denying the horrors which people perpetrate upon one another and the horrors that are suffered. And as therapists, God knows, we must always give lots of room for the story of "what happened" to be told. At the same time, however, we do well to factor what Jung called the "innate sensitiveness" of the subject into the equation. [24] Outward happenings do not affect all alike. What traumatizes one person may be quite indifferent to another. It is sometimes hard to say if a traumatic event has inscribed itself upon the soul or if the soul's sensitiveness has out-pictured itself in a traumatically-rendered scene. And then there is the whole issue of how events are construed by the subject. As Marcel Proust put this, "everyone has his own way of being betrayed, as he has his own way of catching cold." [25]

Besides what happens to us we have our own peculiar ways of being subject to these happenings. Just as it is our way of catching cold that gives the cold virus its bad name, so, too, it is our way of construing events that leads us to succumb to our history as to a nightmare. Though events may seem external to us, they only become experiences proper in accordance with a psychic *a priori* factor, which we unconsciously project upon them. This factor, in which our unique peculiarity or innate sensitiveness is rooted, being *a priori*, can only be experienced, if at all, after itself, in hindsight, through projection upon external events. Events, it follows, provide an "endopsychic perception" (to borrow an expression from Freud) of our own narcissism, and serve our narcissism as selfobjects regardless of whether we idealize them as having had a facilitating influence or denigrate them as pernicious impingements.

"We must never forget," writes Jung in an early paper in which he critiques the trauma theory,

> that the world is, in the first place, a subjective phenomenon. *The impressions we receive from these accidental happenings are also our own doing.* It is not true that the impressions are forced on us unconditionally; our own predisposition conditions the impression. [26]

It is not events, happenings, calamities, and accidents, which are determinate for the psyche, but our experience of them as this experience is mediated by our narcissistic predisposition or self-determining, self-unfolding substance. Events, that is to say, do not *cause* our experience of them. On the contrary, inasmuch as subjectivity and experience are a function of *a priori* psychic factors, these come before events in a manner that provides for their very eventfulness. [27] Like God, the unmoved mover or first cause, [28] the narcissistic ground of our experience creates the meaning of events, causal and noncausal, organizing them, via the archetypes, into synchronistic perceptual patterns which Coleridge, defining perception, called "the repetition in the finite mind of the eternal act of creation in the infinite I Am." [29] Any event that impinges upon our narcissism is instantaneously and unconsciously apperceived by this "uncreated" predisposition in terms of the archetypal idea of an originating act or divine fiat. And it is this that makes the trauma-theory so numinously persuasive. Narcissism, having in our day lost the esteem that it had when it was mirrored in the mighty images of religion, now moves upon the face of causal accounts of the soul's wounding even as the spirit of God once moved upon the face of the deeps. But it is not the otherness of impinging events or the misuse of us by others that wounds our narcissism — at least not in the first place. On the contrary, it is our dislocation from our own supra-personal otherness that does so. The soul, like Narcissus, longs to fall in love with itself, with itself as other, in the pool of religious images. But that pool has dried up. The images have faded. Events now reign supreme.

Is it to events, then, that we now must turn for mirroring? Perhaps we can glimpse in events a reflection of what the soul brings with it. Perhaps we can find in events, or more precisely, in the uniqueness of the self-experience, which provides for their eventfulness, the otherness of the self, that suprapersonal aspect of our narcissism from which the ego-tistical sublime of the me-generation, impoverished of symbolism, has been dislocated.

"In religious experience," writes Jung, "man comes face to face with a psychically overwhelming Other . . . Only something overwhelming, no matter what form of expression it uses, can challenge the whole man and force him to react as a whole."[30] Let us make the same claim for the events of life as Jung makes for religious experience. Let us, that is to say, claim all events for soul, noting how our narcissistic essence unveils itself as the experience from which their eventfulness arises. In so doing we again follow Jung,

> To this day God is the name by which I designate all things which cross my wilful path violently and recklessly, all things which upset my subjective views, plans and intentions and change the course of my life for better or worse.[31]

By relating to the events of his life in an I-Thou fashion, Jung redis-covered, in the midst of our present age of "impoverished symbolism," the gods, which, "as psychic factors . . . archetypes of the unconscious,"[32] give meaning to life. God, as the supra-personal aspect of our narcissism or ar-chetypal image of the self, is revealed to us in and through our experience of the otherness of events. Like the bush, which burned and yet was not consumed, the events of our lives present to us, if only in a sunken fashion, the trace of an imperishable essence of supreme identity even as the God who called Moses from the burning bush identified Himself with a name that is as much ours as His: "I AM WHO I AM" (Ex. 3:14).

1. Sigmund Freud, *An Outline of Psychoanalysis*, trans. J. Strachey (London: Hogarth Press, 1949), p. 77.

2. Friedrich Nietzsche, *A Nietzsche Reader*, trans. R.J. Hollingdale (New York: Penguin Books, 1977), p. 260.

3. John Keats, "Ode to Psyche," lines 52–53. In *Selected Poems and Letters*, p. 204.

4. C.G. Jung, CW 5: 654.

5. Friedrich Nietzsche, *The Portable Nietzsche*, ed. and trans. W. Kaufmann (New York: The Viking Press, 1968), pp. 400–401.

6. William Blake, *Selected Poetry and Prose of Blake*, p. 127.

7. Marie Fortune is a minister and the director of the Center for Prevention of Sexual and Domestic Violence in Seattle. She is the author of *Sexual Violence: The Unmentionable Sin*, a book which discusses sexual abuse and assault from a theological and pastoral perspective.

8. Counter-transference is an issue for the clergyperson no less than it is for the psychotherapist. Although "God" is spoken of in the approved manner characteristic of a particular denomination or faith, the clergyperson and believer may simultaneously use the term to propitiate events in the past, present, or future whose only claim to sacredness is that they have been, or threaten to be, traumatic.

9. Cited by John Bowlby, *Separation: Anxiety and Anger*, vol. 2 of *Attachment and Loss* (Harmondsworth: Penguin Books, 1975), p. 207.

10. Sigmund Freud, "Psycho-Analytic Notes Upon an Autobiographical Account of a Case of Paranoia (*Dementia Paranoides*)," in CP 3: 448–49.

11. Ibid., p. 452.

12. W.G. Niederland, "Schreber: Father and Son," *Psychoanalytic Quarterly* 28 (1959): 151–169, and W.G. Niederland, "The 'Miracled-up' World of Schreber's Childhood," *Psychoanalytic Study of the Child*, 14 (1959): 383–413.

13. Sigmund Freud, "Constructions in Analysis" (1937), in CP, 5: 369.

14. Sigmund Freud, *Totem and Taboo and Other Works*, in *The Standard Edition of the Complete Psychological Works of Sigmund Freud*, ed. James Strachey, 24 vols. (London: Hogarth Press 1953-74), 13: 144. All further references to *The Standard Edition* (*SE*) will be cited by volume and page numbers.

15. C.G. Jung, *Memories, Dreams, Reflections*, p. 39.

16. Sigmund Freud and C.G. Jung *The Freud/Jung Letters: The Correspondence between Sigmund Freud and C.G. Jung*, ed. W. McGuire, trans. R. Manheim & R.F.C. Hull (Princeton: Princeton University Press, 1974), p. 95.

17. Ibid.

18. "By 'archetype' I can refer only to the phenomenal archetype, that which manifests itself in images. The noumenal archetype per se cannot by definition be presented so that nothing whatsoever can be posited of it.

In fact whatever one does say about the archetype per se is a conjecture already governed by an archetypal image. This means that the archetypal image precedes and determines the metaphysical hypothesis of a noumenal archetype." James Hillman, "On the Necessity of Abnormal Psychology," in *Facing the Gods* (Dallas: Spring Publications, 1980), p. 33, n. 6.

19. Ibid., p. 10.

20. Morton Kelsey, *God, Dreams, and Revelation* (Minneapolis: Augsburg Publishing House, 1974), p. 23.

21. Sigmund Freud, "On the Sexual Theories of Children," CP 2: 69.

22. C.G. Jung, CW 14: 659.

23. C.G. Jung, CW 9.1: 50.

24. C.G. Jung, CW 4: 397–99.

25. Cited by Alfred Margulies in *The Empathic Imagination* (New York: W.W. Norton, 1989), p. 92.

26. C.G. Jung, CW 4: 400.

27. This "beforeness" is not temporal but ontological, a beforeness, which is not in time, but above time, in *illo tempore*.

28. Jung: "The ego stands to the self as the moved to the mover, or as object to subject, because the determining factors which radiate out from the self [projected upon the events of life] surround the ego on all sides and are therefore supraordinate to it. The self, like the unconscious, is an *a priori* existent out of which the ego evolves." CW 11: 391.

29. Samuel Taylor Coleridge, *Biographia Literaria*, ed. J. Engel & W.J. Bate (Princeton: Bollingen Series LXXV, Princeton University Press, 1984), vol. 1, p. 304.

30. C.G. Jung, CW 10: 655.

31. Cited in Edward Edinger, *Ego and Archetype* (Boston & London: Shambhala, 1992), p. 101.

32. C.G. Jung, CW 9.1: 50.

# chapter five

# THE TRAUMA OF INCARNATION AND

# THE SUR-NATURAL SOUL

## Breaking the Spell

With an inverted sense of wonder, psyche asks: "what is *is*?" Immediately stupefied, it dummies down its query, if only by re-directing its question from *Being* in general to *beings* in their particularity. With this move (think of the infant held in its mother's eyes), the sense of stupefaction lessens. Things stand forth. Faces throng around. The question about is-ness loses its traumatic intensity. But never entirely . . .

"[N]ot quite can you call him away from that sinister company," writes Rilke,

> Truly, he tries, he escapes, and nestles disburdened
>     into your secret heart, where he takes and is newly begun.
> But, did he ever begin himself?
> Mother, you made him small, it was you who began him;
>     to you he was new, and over the young eyes you bent down a world
>     that was friendly and staved off the strange.
> Where, O where are the years when you simply,
>     by stepping in front of it,
>     screened with your slender figure the seething abyss?
> Much you did hide from him thus; the room that was creepy at
>     night you made harmless, and out of your heart full of refuge
>     you mingled a humaner space with his night-space. [1]

An essential tension is captured by Rilke in these lines. As welcoming as the world may be (and, of course, even more so when it is not) moments remain when the mediating action that had "staved off the strange" no longer does so. In these moments — Wordsworth spoke of "spots of time" — the question at the back of things again breaks through. *Mysterium tremendum et facinans*. Subject to strange resistances, we are returned to that manger which long in advance of itself was already this present uncomfortable pew.

"As I go on in this life, day by day," writes Robert Louis Stevenson,

> I become more of a bewildered child. I cannot get used to this
> world, to procreation, to heredity, to sight, to hearing; the com-
> monest things are a burthen. The prim, polite surface of life,
> and the broad, bawdy, and orgiastic — or maenadic — founda-
> tions, form a spectacle to which no habit reconciles me. [2]

Does the great novelist show himself to have been in need of an analyst? Perhaps — but of what kind? With regards to the bewilderment that
children feel with respect to the prim, polite, bawdy and orgiastic, Freud, of
course, has had much to say. "Three Essays on Sexuality," "From the History
of an Infantile Neurosis," "On Narcissism": surely there is a receiving blanket for the bewildered Stevenson in these texts.

But what of Jung? What has he had to say on this subject? Sharing
Stevenson's child-like bewilderment, Jung writes:

> [Freudian psychology] points no way that leads beyond the in-
> exorable cycle of biological events. In despair we would have
> to cry out with St. Paul: "Wretched man that I am, who will
> deliver me from the body of this death?" And the spiritual
> man in us comes forward, shaking his head, and says in Faust's
> words: "Thou art conscious only of the single urge," namely of
> the fleshy bond leading back to father and mother or forward
> to the children that have sprung from our flesh — "incest" with
> the past and "incest" with the future, the original sin of per-
> petuation of the "family romance."

Having thrown down the gauntlet (in his *Three Essays,* Freud had declared recognition of the Oedipus complex to be "the shibboleth that distinguishes the adherents of psychoanalysis from its opponents" [3]), Jung
continues:

> There is nothing that can free us from this bond except that
> opposite urge of life, the spirit. It is not the children of the
> flesh, but the "children of God," who know freedom. In Ernst
> Barlach's tragedy *The Dead Day*, the mother-daemon says at the
> end: "The strange thing is that man will not learn that God is

his father." That is what Freud would never learn, and what all those who share his outlook forbid themselves to learn. At least, they never find the key to this knowledge. Theology does not help those who are looking for the key, because theology demands faith, and faith cannot be made: it is in the truest sense a gift of grace. We moderns are faced with the necessity of rediscovering the life of the spirit; we must experience it anew for ourselves. It is the only way in which to break that spell that binds us to the cycle of biological events. [4]

Jung's references to "the cycle of biological events," St. Paul's to "the body of this death," Stevenson's to the "spectacle [of life] to which no habit reconciles [him]," these, along with Rilke's images of "the seething abyss," "night-space" and a "sinister company" from which the mother cannot completely shield her child, may remind us of the views of another analyst: D.W. Winnicott. "It must be conceded," Winnicott writes,

> . . . that there are very roughly speaking two kinds of human being, those who do not carry around with them a significant experience of mental breakdown in earliest infancy and those who do carry around with them such an experience and who must therefore flee from it, flirt with it, fear it, and to some extent be always preoccupied with the threat of it. [5]

Doubtless, Winnicott is correct in pointing out that many people carry around with them, in their otherwise adult personalities, sectors of madness that were instilled in them by early trauma. In his paper "Fear of Breakdown," he writes insightfully about the anticipatory anxiety to which such people are continuously subject. [6] Filled with stressful innervations and chaotic impressions, these people unwittingly project their anxiety-laden protomemories upon contemporary situations, such that a dreadful feeling of impending doom forecloses their ability to make use of what life holds for them in the present. Terrified, often at precisely those junctures that others find wondrous, they defend themselves in bizarre and self-defeating ways. But their paranoid manoeuvring does not bring safety. On the contrary, in the manner of a film of the urban nightmare genre, a version of what is unconsciously feared is recreated by the very effort to keep it at bay. Finally, a crisis point is reached, the goodness at hand being too much to be trusted. In moments such as these (Freud spoke of "the negative therapeutic reaction"), Winnicott's interpretation — that what the patient dreads has already happened, long ago in infancy — combined with his other important insight — that psyche actively restages its traumas as part of a process of bringing about an emotional settlement with them — can be just the right medicine.

But here, let the seductions of theory not seduce us into thinking that the mother-analyst can entirely "stave off the strange" any more than the mother in Rilke's poem can. Just as Freud said that there is always something about the sexual instinct that remains unsatisfied, so there is something within the infant psyche that never feels properly responded to or held. Analyzing the traumas of his early life, Freud always found that for each one there was another preceding it. The impression arising from this was of an infinite regress. Reflecting upon this, our focus may move, as Freud's did, from the outwardness of traumatic events to the inwardness of the subject's prone-ness to be traumatized.

Deep at the a back of things, suspended amidst the perturbing influences of the world like the simple vesicle of Freud's *Beyond the Pleasure Principle*, lies our metaphysical substance or essential narcissism. Far from being a *tabula rasa* devoid of qualities, this essential, or as we may also designate it, higher narcissism brings the imperative of its uniqueness to the world. But uniqueness cannot maintain itself without resistance. As noted at the outset, as wondrous as the world may be, there is also a need to tighten-up against it for a time. In a passage that can be read with reference to this, Jung writes of the psyche's tendency to produce images of a traumatized or abandoned child, even when no real trauma, in the ordinary sense, has occurred: "The initial stage of personal infantilism presents the picture of an 'abandoned' or 'misunderstood' and unjustly treated child with overweening pretensions." [7] Following upon this, Jung writes of a second identification, "the epiphany of the hero [which] . . . shows itself in a corresponding inflation: the colossal pretension grows into a conviction that one is something extraordinary, or else the impossibility of the pretension ever being fulfilled only proves one's own inferiority, which is favorable to the role of the heroic sufferer (a negative inflation)." [8]

Certainly a mother's job, as Rilke so beautifully portrays, is to protect her child from the arrows and slings that can be so damaging to his narcissism. However, it is also the case, as the poet conveys, that she cannot quite call her child back from the sinister company that his overweening pretensions or essentialistic inklings keep with the world that has preceded his beginning with her. She cannot. Nor can or should analysis. For what Rilke refers to with this menacing image is nothing other than the daemonic source of the soul's character and calling. [9]

Writing with reference to what we may now interchangeably refer to as "sinister company," "daemonic source," "overweening pretensions," "essentialist inkings," "archetypal imperative," "individuation urge" and "destiny drive," Jung avers that

> The infinity of the child's preconscious soul may disappear with it, or it may be preserved. The remnants of the child-soul in the adult are his best and worst qualities; at all events they are the mysterious *spiritus rector* of our weightiest deeds and of our individual destinies, whether we are conscious of it or not. It is they which make kings or pawns of the insignificant figures who move about on the checker-board of life, turning some poor devil of a casual father into a ferocious tyrant, or a silly goose of an unwilling mother into a goddess of fate. For behind every individual father there stands the primordial image of the Father, and behind the fleeting personal mother the magical figure of the Magna Mater. These archetypes of the collective psyche, whose power is magnified in immortal works of art and in the fiery tenets of religion, are the dominants that rule the preconscious soul of the child and, when projected upon the human parents, lend them a fascination which often assumes monstrous proportions. [10]

"Not quite can you call him back from that sinister company . . ." Rilke, here, is to our Jungian point. As valuable as Winnicott's views regarding early trauma are to us each day in our practices, we must also push off from these even as Freud pushed off from the seduction theory. While not failing to attend to the pathogenic effects of sexual abuse when it occurred, Freud, it will be recalled, withdrew the seduction theory. Drive fantasies, he came to believe, could disturb and confuse the developing child in a manner that created a picture very like that of abuse at the hands of a perverted adult. Our move in the pages that follow will be similar to this. While remaining concerned about the deleterious effects of trauma in general, and early trauma in particular, our task shall be to reach inward, into the interiority of the subject, to find that fabulous spirit for whom incarnation can be so tight and traumatic a squeeze.

## Why and Because

The most basic trauma of all is the trauma of *incarnation.* By *incarnation* I do not mean the vicissitudes a baby suffers while navigating the birth-canal — the so-called birth-trauma of Otto Rank. I mean, rather, the overwhelming nature of our given reality. The doctor may count up our fingers and toes when we are born, but even if he pronounces that we are all there, the *form* of our existence is, nonetheless, irrational and arbitrary. "Why five fingers and not six or three? Why do we need to defecate, to procreate, to eat and breath? Why Mommy? Why? Why?"

Perhaps humanity can be divided into two groups: the group that are satisfied with an amused "because" and the group that are not.

The first group, the group that easily adjusts to the arbitrary, irrational character of existence, is typically perceived to be the most natural and healthy. Although, in truth, their lives are simply a collection of irrationalities, they can experience their existence as rational, so long as its irrationality is congruent with the irrationality of the world itself. Existential conflicts do not occur to these cast-iron constitutions. As children they grow like weeds; as adults they seem to succeed in the world; as parents they answer every "why?" with "because." As each successive generation grows up as unconscious as the last, the *congruence* within this transgenerational transmission process of anti-awareness paradoxically lends the illusion of consciousness, meaning and purpose to life. But when the preservation of the species, the cycle of biology, and the universal repetition of the Oedipus complex suffice as the meaning of life, the "because" has triumphed.

The second group, the group that are less identified with the imme-diacy of their incarnational life and who cannot be reconciled to the ir-rationality of existence by an amused "because," are typically perceived as being more or less neurotic. The given world never quite makes sense to these people. Eating, drinking, defecating, and procreating seem, at best, a servitude to the irrational. The question "why" continues to be an obses-sion, perhaps even distorting itself into a case of hypochondria or para-noid insecurity. With their "peculiar" behavior and "neurotic" reticence, individuals of this second group seem "irrational" to the radiant members of the first group who are so absorbed into the arbitrariness of existence that it does not seem the least bit arbitrary or irrational to them. Looked askance at by their more happily incarnated neighbors, the members of the second group can readily reply to this with a critical gaze of their own. How brutish, vulgar, insensitive and callously vital the members of the first group look from their perspective! As the saying goes, though we are all in the gutter at least some of us are looking at the stars.

Between the two groups there is an exchange of traffic. It frequent-ly happens, for example, that a member of the first group can fall from his pristine state of grace into the company of his less happily incarnated brothers. Perhaps some overwhelming event befalls him from some irra-tional quarter, disinheriting him of the world which had previously seemed so straightforward and true. Perhaps he sustains an injury or contracts an incurable disease. Perhaps a parent dies or his family is divided by a di-vorce. "Why me?" he cries, "why me?" But no longer can a "because" serve as a magic answer.

Traffic going the other direction often proceeds by means of the con-solations of religion. Those souls who feel like strangers in a strange land — "in this world, but not of it" — often find in the illusions of religion suf-ficient rationale to make the absurdity of the world stomachable.

But is there not another answer to the soul's "why" than the "because" of nature and the "because" of religion? There is. This other option is re-creation, culture-making, soul-making.

The act of re-creation, the act of giving our own form to the chaos of existence, takes us out of the traumatic parent/child rhetoric of "why"

and "because." Now, if we think of this in isolation it seems all too heroic: every person an originating artist. What I have in mind when I speak
of soul-making, however, has more to do with a *re-engagement of culture*. For
some, soul-making may indeed mean originating; for most people, however, it means giving the developments of culture their psychological as-
sent — claiming the changes, evaluating them and instinctualizing them
accordingly. Today we live in the dispensation of a long history of other
makers. The "whys" and "becauses" that once punctuated the traumatic
absurdity of existence have been increasingly absorbed into the free verse
of man's own creating will.

After Jesus told his disciples that "it is easier for a camel to go through
the eye of a needle than for a rich man to enter the kingdom of God," Peter
replied, "Behold, we have left everything and followed You; what then will
there be for us?" Jesus answered Peter's question by promising that "you
who have followed Me, in the regeneration when the Son of Man will sit
of His glorious throne, you also shall sit upon thrones judging the twelve
tribes of Israel:

> And everyone who has left houses or brothers or sisters or fa-
> ther or mother or children or farms for My name's sake, shall
> receive many times as much, and shall inherit eternal life.
> But many who are first will be last; and the last, first.
> (Matthew 19:24, 27–30)

If we read this passage gnostically, taking the promise of inheriting
eternal life to mean the tapping of our age-old cultural inheritance, we
discover a curious relationship between absence and presence. Again and
again biography places before us examples of lives in which the first have
become last, where the second born succeeded the first, where the needle's
eye of a subtle psychological inheritance was disinheritance.

The absurd event we heartily except as members of the first group
enters the mind as a content of consciousness, or the soul as an experience,
only when we lose our unquestioning grip upon it. When we fall into the
second group, the group of the dispossessed, what we have lost becomes
immensely present in its absence. The dead parent, the lost love, the faded beauty — precisely by virtue of being dead, lost, and faded — are re-

leased from their literal encasement in the absurd and become metaphors. Although still particular, they "float" as categories, perspectives, integrities of soul, intelligences, angels. Trauma is the eye of the needle through which we enter the kingdom of culture. Through the thorns in our flesh we re-engage culture, body it forth anew, evaluate and instinctualize it.

The boy without a father, for example, can be fathered by the culture. Through the eye of his wound he can entertain a variety of fathering styles, most of which are entirely invisible to the boys of the first group who play ball after supper with a man whose genetic resemblance to them masks the absurdity of the whole human enterprise. A phenomenologist of fathering, the fatherless son may even make first place out of last. Watching television programs, reading books, evaluating his mother's lovers and the fathers and step-fathers of other boys, he may even gain an uncanny prowess as a man against what seem unlikely odds. Or drawn back by strange dreams into the "sinister company" of his unmediated archetypal expectations, he may break windows, commits crimes or become in intellectual iconoclast. In either case, he finds *presence* through the needle's eye of its absence. His inheritance is a subtle inheritance: the experience of "fathering" as an event of the soul, discontinuous, yes, but ubiquitous for all that.

## Arbitrary Particulars

Wordsworth knew about the "be-cusses" and be-causes" of life into which we have been crammed by that "homely Nurse [who] doth all she can / To make her foster child, her Inmate Man, / Forget the glories he hath known, / And the imperial palace whence he came. [11] He knew how quickly the soul, given over to events it is unable to alter, becomes dislocated from the "vision splendid" of its imaginal power. In his poems, he poignantly describes the insidious process by which the play of the mind becomes restricted by the brute circumstances that were given with its birth.

> And the Babe leaps on his Mother's arm —
> I hear, I hear, with joy I hear!
> — But there's a Tree, of many, one,

A single Field which I have looked upon,
Both of them speak of something that is gone:
   The Pansy at my feet
   Doth the same tale repeat:
Whither is fled the visionary gleam?
Where is it now, the glory and the dream? [12]

The arbitrary particulars of our incarnational life traumatize awareness. The sheer concreteness and outwardness of existence quickly forecloses the "visionary gleam . . . the glory and the dream." Each particular
thing that we arbitrarily encounter commits us to the objective sphere in
a manner that has a determining effect upon all subsequent encounters.
Again, as Freud and Breuer put it, "any impression which the nervous system has difficulty dealing with by means of associative thinking or by motor reaction becomes a psychical trauma." [13]

Life itself is traumatic to soul. Simply by virtue of becoming actually
something or someone to somebody, the soul ceases to be potentially anything and everything to anyone and everybody. Predicated to the few that
make up its actual life, the soul loses sight of its immortal attributes and
becomes a function of the lowest terms it holds in common with the other
beings with which it shares life's stage. "Fad[ing] into the light of common
day" (or deigning to join what we now called the "dysfunctional family")
such, evidently, is the price of becoming real.

But the vision-darkening prose of incarnation can still give way to
poetry. Though "our birth," as Wordsworth writes, "is but a sleep and
a forgetting," it is still possible to explore while "sleeping" — through a
dream, a poem, or the dialectical bent of our minds — what incarnation
had required soul to forget. Though our lives are ultimately embedded
in circumstances beyond our power to alter, *we can still to speculate, fanta-
size, and imagine.* These imaginal modes provide the soul with access to
the psychic potentialities which incarnation into the actualities of life
would otherwise have caused it to relinquish. Reflected into themselves
in these ways, the tight spots into which we have been incarnationally
squeezed bring forth from their own narrow confines a vision of the
Beyond. Though we remain predicated to the few that make up our actual life, it is now as if the infinite were at play through our connection

to them. Not the lowest common terms but the highest is the promise of the imaginal mode.

Negativizing the naive relation to the world reflectively into itself, Christ, the great exemplar of a *sublated* incarnation asks, "What profits a man if he gain the whole world and lose the kingdom?" While we certainly must be in the world to be real, it is by not being totally of the world that we force it into truth. Just as the "Risen Crucified" did not come "to bring peace on earth . . . but a sword," so, too, must our becoming bring, not merely the peace of accommodation, but the sword of resistance to the brute contingencies of the otherwise truthless real. Entering the fray of the arbitrarily-given (if only as the soldiers of our symptoms), each of us must bear as arms all that incarnation would require us to give up. Each of us, that is to say, must weigh in as that "infinitesimal grain"[14] which our scruples, inhibitions, and oddities are, wrestling with life's contingencies as both Jacob and angel at once.

At the beginning of his ode, Wordsworth declares "the child to be father to the man." Seconding this insight, Coleridge defined the task of the poet as "carry[ing] on the feelings of childhood into the powers of Manhood."[15] Radicalizing these statements, let us reach back behind the childhood to which these poets refer to the *bardo* of pre-existence. It is the *sensitivities* rooted in this realm that must be carried forward in the face of life's contingencies. Not only the child we once were, but that placental twin or angel that we always already are must be carried forward as well.

What, we may now ask (in light the foregoing reflections) is the "clinical picture" a picture of — a trauma or an angel? Regarded imaginatively the former of these, our traumas, can be thought of as the concretized out-picturing of what the latter inwardly perceives. Our traumas, that is to say, would not be what as traumas they are had not our narcissism occult reaches as vast as the great welter of perturbing vicissitudes reaching it from without. Demanding much more than a "because," the soul in its greater narcissism turns fact into truth. Suspended amidst the perturbing stimuli of the world like the simple vesicle of Freud's theorizing, it interiorizes these stimuli mythopoeically into themselves even as it associatively and dissociatively brings forth an image from them.[16]

Such is its image-making power that Jung regarded the psyche to be "the world's pivot." [17] The idea here is that as the traumas of the real impinge they simultaneously tear open an inner world constituted of imaginal responses that are not wholly derivative. Rivalling the vastness of the universe without — with its atoms, planetary bodies, and traumatic laws of motion — a universe within asserts itself. "I can only gaze with wonder and awe at the depths and heights of our psychic nature," writes Jung, recovering the "vision splendid" for our time in light of this recognition:

> Its non-spatial universe conceals an untold abundance of images which have accumulated over millions of years of living development and become fixed in the organism. My consciousness is like an eye that penetrates to the most distant spaces, yet it is the psychic non-ego that fills them with non-spatial images. And these images are not pale shadows, but tremendously powerful psychic factors. The most we may be able to do is misunderstand them, but we can never rob them of their power by denying them. Beside this picture I would like to place the spectacle of the starry heavens at night, for the only equivalent of the universe within is the universe without; and just as I reach this world through the medium of the body, so I reach that world through the medium of the psyche. [18]

## Symptoms As Family

Let us imagine a "family" therapy that is less interested in family dynamics and their enhancement as a preventative or therapeutic factor than in the individuation value of the symptoms to which family members are subject. Although it is a convention of family therapy and family-oriented psychotherapy to view symptoms interpersonally, for instance, as contracts between people, symptoms can also be imagined as having a spiritual aspect that is post-Oedipal and extra-familial. Even when it is clearly evident that a symptom is a function of enmeshed relationships crossing generational boundaries, it is also an inner experience of an individual and as such may be discontinuous with, a pushing off from, the family milieu that has so obviously contributed to it.

As lived and felt experiences symptoms have a shameful, alienating quality that often makes the symptom-bearer withdraw into secrecy and stand alone — a mystery to himself and others. This aloneness, however, is at the same time the opposite of itself, for the symptom is also an "other." Indeed, it might even be called a most significant other given that his relationship to it immediately rivals the relationship that he has had with friends and family members, sometimes to the point that it becomes the most important relationship in his life.

To be related to a symptom is to be radically related to oneself, the dissociative otherness of the symptom asymmetrically mirroring a depth of subjectivity not previously known. What was at first suffered and resisted as alienation — a sense of being different or of being a "freak" — gradually reveals itself as an angelic face of one's own unknowable essence. And, inasmuch as the symptom is experienced as an ego-alien content welling up from within the subject, one's relationship to it suggests a relationship to an immanent and, yet, transcendent aspect of the psyche.

This accords with experience. Like gods or devils, symptoms can be over-powering. In a passage that presages his later research into the spiritual aspect of the unconscious, a passage dealing with especially severe psychopathological symptoms, Jung writes: "The psyche does not merely *react*, it gives its own specific answer to the influences at work upon it." [19] To grasp the spiritual significance of a symptom for our lives we must recognize that it is not merely a reaction to such outer influences as family dynamics, though this may certainly be one of its valances. More than that, it is a *reply* or *answer* to those influences, an answer, moreover, arising from our own specific nature as this is rooted in the otherness of the objective psyche. Addressing us as if it were a God, the symptom demands submission, obedience, and sacrifice to a side of our nature, which must now be dialectically deployed to counter external impingements or to redress internal exclusivities (i.e., our one-sidedness attitudes). Unwilling to leave "houses or brothers or sisters or father or mother or children or farms" (Matthew 19:29) for the sake of our symptoms, and yet, unable to do otherwise, we are compelled by our symptoms to a regenerative form of existence which is experienced negatively, at first, as the ruin of our family life and childhood. Cursing our symptoms with the same breath as we curse the family members whom we blame for causing them, we fail to recognize that although these symptoms have, in many ways, destroyed our childhoods, they have also raised us. In their own incredibly individual and individuating way the symptoms have also provided shelter, a home away from home — even though we may at first have tried to run away from this home too by trying to be normal. The amazing thing is not that families are dysfunctional and that family members suffer as a result. The amazing thing is how resilient we are. It is quite as if we are archetypally engineered, through thousands of years of evolution, to survive the dysfunctional family. As odd as our parents may be, there is a sense that we've met them before. Not just at birth, but at every stage of our development, we measure our mothers and fathers, brothers and sisters, husbands and wives, friends and enemies against this primordial sense of *déjà vu*. No wonder they fail us! No wonder that we, like Freud's beloved patient, the Wolfman, become the feral children of our symptoms! We are so equipped to survive our life in family that their failure of us is almost an initiatory necessity within which our love for ourselves and our love for them travails. For until they fail us, until, that is to say, the curtain falls on the family romance, we do not really love or hate them at all, but rather, the Gods in whose image and likeness we have omnipotently perceived them.

## Chronicity, Individuality, and the Traumatic Soul

Sometimes we cling to our troubles as if the agitating grit at their core were a precious bit of star dust. Although a complex could be discharged, a perversion out-grown, a transference resolved, or an irksome habit given up, these often linger on as the guardians of something exquisitely sensitive, secret, and dear in our narcissism.

It is so from the beginning and from our beginning's beyond. Janus-faced, the nursing babe looks both outward into its mother's eyes and inward to the "infinity of [its] . . . preconscious soul," that "mysterious *spiritus rector* of our weightiest deeds and of our individual destinies . . . ."[20] Small wonder that there is sometimes such struggling in the swaddling bands. Loath to be absorbed into the existing categories of assimilation (given, in part, by our family mythology and cultural surround), we obstinately resist the conventions to which the outwardness of life would recruit us, questioning, thereby, the established methods of turning events into experiences.

Love, of course, is a great mediator and mitigator — especially parental and family love. But as much as we may feel the welcome and protection of the "facilitating environment" that these provide, a hovering something may still hold back, as if to ensure that the apple falls a goodly distance from the tree. Viewed purposively, this holding back and passing strange is part of an effort to critique, on *a priori* grounds, the arbitrary and, yet, collectively approved categories of assimilation and care. Reaching back to the *cogito* of its own anti-Oedipal doubts, the soul clings to the untoward and traumatic for the sake of the angelic "why?" that these raise. To allow an event to be too easily assimilated (or itself to be too readily accepted or held) would be to accept the sugar-coating of a "because," and to the Gnostic sensibility the metaphysical consolation of a "because" merely adds insult to injury. And all this is to say nothing, yet, of bad handling!

We are arriving at a paradoxical formulation. We have been defining trauma throughout these pages as an overwhelming event that has a determining effect upon our consciousness and life. Now we are suggesting, on the model of a monkey wrench in the works, that a particular trauma can actually open consciousness. Just by virtue of its being something that happens specifically to us, the traumatic event has the effect of disturbing the anxiety-avoiding accommodations which we have soullessly made to the wider trauma of our incarnational surround. Suddenly we do have extra fingers, a myriad of riddling symptoms with which to sign. As symbolic as they are diabolical, these inhibiting and life-critiquing symptoms are the guardians of the self's most sensitive core and a larger-than-life out-picturing of the little milligram that we each metaphysically are.[21]

Partly, what a trauma confers upon us is a shameful sense of individuality. Something has happened to us that made us unlike anyone else we know, different, even, from our next of kin. Or turning this around, our preternatural uniqueness finds in the event we call "traumatic" the Other in which its ego-transcending immanence is figured. *"The experience of the self,"* writes Jung, *"is always a defeat for the ego."* [22]

A few lines from Coleridge touch upon the logic that is at work here. Writing with reference to what he variously calls the Sum, I am, spirit, self, and self-consciousness, Coleridge states that ". . . it is a subject which becomes a subject by the act of constructing itself objectively to itself; but which never is an object except for itself and only so far as by the same act it becomes a subject; it may be described therefore as a perpetual self-duplication of one and the same power into object and subject." [23] Writing in a similar vein to Coleridge, Jung states that ". . . *in religious experience man comes face to face with a psychically overwhelming Other.*" A few lines later he continues, "Only something overwhelming, no matter what form of expression it uses, can challenge the whole man and force him to react as a whole." [24]

Often it is less the specific calamity that we cannot absorb — the rape, the acne, the abuse, the accident — but the *individuality* these events underline, particularize, and abandon us to. Called forth by challenges and contingencies on a scale not previously known, our little self or familiar ego is at first dwarfed by the larger personality emerging from it. Said another way, the immensity of the soul's response can be just as traumatic as the event that has triggered it. Resilience, too, can be a trauma.

In his essay, "Concerning Rebirth," Jung speaks of moments in life when "'One becomes Two,' and the greater figure, which one always was but which remained invisible, appears to the lesser personality with the force of a revelation." [25] The moments to which Jung refers correspond, on the one hand, to the wellknown turning points of life and, on the other, to the defining moments of our most individual fate. Now, when this unfolding of the one into two is distributed interpersonally, a process develops in which we "meet ourselves . . . in a thousand disguises on the path of life." [26] Capturing something of this drama in a case study dealing with the dream of a boy who feared his father, Jung writes: "For the boy, the father is an anticipation of his own masculinity, conflicting with his wish to remain infantile." [27] Like Jacob wrestling with the angel at the ford, so also must we wrestle — with the aversive events that assail us from without, the mantic depths of our narcissism, and one another — unable though we may be to know with any certainty which is which.

The individuality of the soul can never be finally absorbed. This is not simply because traumas overwhelm the categories of assimilation with which the soul tries to incorporate them. The opposite is also true: the soul is overwhelmed with itself, with its own intrinsic character structure. Dialectically refusing the consolations of the only natural order (the object relationships that are associated with healthy development), the soul seeks to retain its connection to a part of itself that cannot live on the earth at all. Now, the "cannot" here does not refer to a positive lack but to a negative fullness or plenty. It is through being reflected into itself in terms of the part of the soul that cannot live on the earth that "earth" becomes "world."

## Refusing Incarnation

Symptoms are the soul's way disincarnating itself from its encasement in the arbitrary order of the simply given world. Phobias, eating disorders, sexual dysfunctions, etc.: in all these troubles the natural or "normal" state of our being has been disrupted. Behaviors that were once simply spontaneous aspects of our arbitrary animality become self-conscious, reflective, inhibited, objects of concern and worry. It is by losing our capacity to maintain an erection, experience an orgasm, eat food, or walk in the marketplace, etc., that we become human. When the monkey lost its tail and fell out of its tree, it stood up and became Man.

We regain what we lose only by re-creating it. After we experience the failure of what had hitherto functioned automatically and unconsciously we can never again take it for granted. With the development of a symptom innocence is lost. The penis will not erect again until we re-invent it. No matter how much the patient tries, he cannot will back its old spontaneity. But if he takes his lead from the symptomatic state of his penis, he may penetrate out of its old mythology precisely by means of its flaccidity. As the penis is re-invented (by changing the values and attitudes surrounding it) it loses its arbitrary animality and becomes part of human intercourse. Now, paradoxically, spontaneity can return to it, at least until the possibilities of its new mythology have been exhausted. In our soul-making we need never fear: a recurrence can always happen should we need a new orientation.

## Parapraxis

The failed performances of our day to day life, the omissions of memory and slips of the tongue — the whole gamut of miscarried behaviors that Freud referred to as "the psychopathology of everyday life" — could these not be gnostic seizures at the sight of the incarnation's shadow? As soon as we start to act, as soon as we commit ourselves to an event or plan of action, a heretic moment trips us up as if some unconscious will in us were refusing incarnation.

Freud explained failed performances in terms of conflicting currents of the libido. The words that slip uncensored over the tongue, in Freud's view, bespeak the presence of rival drives. But perhaps failed performances have more to do with a gnostic resistance to being locked up into the chain of events which performance completions would inaugurate. Viewed from this perspective, the psychopathology of everyday life is a psychological or theological counter-movement that refuses to forfeit the polymorphous and indeterminate pleasures of the eternal child for the reality ego of historicized adulthood. Or, to put this more dialectically (for, of course, mature into adults we must), it is as if our adulthood's reality ego must stumble over its words and say silly or embarrassing things if it is to enter the Kingdom by means of that child who is reputed to be the Kingdom's gate or entrance point.

The slip-ups and calamities from which we sometimes say an angel saved us — could these have been occasioned by an angel? Is there a child above us who watches over the child below? And as we grow up in compliance, taking on more and more responsibility, does this other child grow *down*, as Hillman has suggested, [28] to help make sure that our compliance is not too much of a compromise?

Perhaps our resistance to the reality principle of corporate adult-hood is not only the expression of something childish in us that must be overcome. Perhaps it is the expression of something archetypal, childlike, and inspirational that must never be entirely abandoned. Our *faux pas* may leave us red-faced with embarrassment, but before we regressively restore our former persona let us consider the possibility that the embarrassment which we so rue is actually the luminous glow of our angel's halo.

Significantly, for all its stake in stages of development and in models of psychopathology that think it terms of fixation points and derailments of the developmental process, psychoanalysis shares with gnosticism the concern that the adulthood which its patients have achieved may be in the status of a false self. Returning via the developmental perspective to the child which the patient was never properly able to be, psychoanaly-sis speaks of itself as sponsoring a benign or therapeutically usable form of regression. Bracketing the developmental metaphor, a gnostic analysis thinks rather of the child of our essential narcissism as the imaginal link to the soul's most essential values. Doubtless, in the consulting room both these ends play off against the middle realm of the soul's making.

But let us return to the psychopathology of everyday life and to the comparison of this with the values of the early gnostics. What the gnostic part of us does as error and mistake, some early sects of gnostics did con-sciously and with pious intent. Wanting to participate as little as possible in the incarnational world in which they believed spirit to be trapped, these gnostics practiced a kind of civil disobedience. In order to free the spirit from material servitude, they broke all the rules and regulations which they felt perpetuated the misbegotten world.

Can children's problems be read against the same background? In his memoirs, Jung mentions a number of occasions in his childhood when he stumbled in his play, some almost fatal:

> There was a fall downstairs, for example, and another fall against the angle of a stove leg. I remember pain and blood, a doctor sewing a wound in my head . . . My mother told me, too, of the time which I was crossing the bridge over the Rhine Falls to Neuhausen. The maid caught me just in time — I already had one leg under the railing and was about to slip through.

*These things point to an unconscious suicidal urge or, it may be, to a fatal*
*resistance to life in this world.* [29]

Later, in the same chapter, a few pages after telling us that his "first
conscious trauma" [30] had to do with the fright he felt at the sight of a
black-robed Jesuit on the road, Jung relates another story of catastroph-
ic resistance or parapraxic gnosticism. While walking past a Catholic
church, the young Jung slipped away from his mother to look inside.
"I just had time to glimpse the big candles on a richly adorned altar . .
. ," he writes, "when I suddenly stumbled on a step and struck my chin
on a piece of iron. I remember that I had a gash that was bleeding badly
when my parents picked me up." [31] Overcoming his embarrassment and
his sense of having done something forbidden, Jung immediately connected this event up with his fear of Jesuits, amongst other things. "It is
their fault that I stumbled and screamed," he thought to himself. While
this is the conclusion he drew at the time, a more general statement from
a later chapter helps to convey our idea about the gnostic resistances and
preternatural nostalgia that children sometimes display in the face of
gravity, the earth, peas and carrots, and parents:

> Children react much less to what grown-ups say than to the
> imponderables in the surrounding atmosphere. The child un-
> consciously adapts himself to them, and this produces in him
> correlations of a compensatory nature. The peculiar "religious"
> ideas that came to me even in my earliest childhood were spon-
> taneous products which can be understood only as reactions to
> my parental environment and to the spirit of the age. [32]

Today, for the most part, we lack the theology necessary to understand the resistances that a heretic part of us always feels with respect
to incarnation. After 2 thousand years of incarnational religion it is almost impossible to see the memory lapses, slips of the tongue, errors of
the pen, and falls upon the stairs as anything more than events in need
of correction, salvation, and cure. But for the gnostic part of us, these
events — or anti-events — are themselves the correction, salvation, and
cure for the imprisonment of the soul in matter, convention, and the
"inexorable cycle of biological events."

## Gnostic Transference

If the soul is "unnatural," a perennial "why?" before the arbitrarity of mere being, what are the "occult" contents of the transference? In the Freudian view, the contents of the transference are the parental imagos. The patient transfers his or her parental complexes onto the therapist and a therapy of re-parenting or de-parenting is then conducted according to the therapist's inclinations. But from a Gnostic, Platonic, alchemical or Wordsworthian point of view, what is being projected onto the therapist in the transference is the naturalistic fallacy into which the soul has been incarnated. By projecting the arbitrary particularity or determinate contingencies of his incarnational life onto the person of the therapist (i.e., the imagos of parents he did not choose), the patient converts those familial chains of cause and effect into images and metaphors of the soul's own choosing. It is precisely because the therapist is not the patient's mother or father that the patient can penetrate out of his mother and father by projecting their particularity onto him. In the transference, the parental imagos shed their historical sense of particularity (the therapist is, after all, *not* the historical parent) and "float" as categories, just as they did when as a young child the patient could still wonder why he was born to his parents and not to others.

In the wrangles of the transference, it is not simply the specific infantile wishes and the specific disappointments that the patient works through. It is the whole problem of incarnation that is confronted. The fierce incest wishes of the transference, the oral aggressiveness and oral greed (and even more the finicky reversal of these), enact a *via negativa*. It is not merely that the "natural" child is continuing in the adult patient to make infantile demands upon the parent whom he projects onto the therapist; rather, it is that the "unnatural soul" is negating the determinate status of the particularity in which it is trapped, exposing this as arbitrary and absurd. When the patient can see as arbitrary the things he once had seen as determinate, and when he can wed this resultant sense of Maya to his own creating will, his provisional life and vicarious religion are over.

A therapy, which aims at soul-making takes the side of the "sur-natural" soul. Its sensibility is like the sensibility of Wordsworth when he wrote in his "Ode: Intimations of Immortality":

> Of Childhood, whether busy or at rest,
> With new-fledged hope still fluttering in his breast —
>     Not for these I raise
>     The song of thanks and praise;
>     But for those obstinate questionings
> Of sense and outward things,
>     Fallings from us, vanishings;
>     Blank misgivings of a Creature
> Moving about in worlds not realized [i.e., not seeming real]
> High instincts before which our mortal Nature
> Did tremble like a guilty Thing surprised;
>     But for those first affections,
>     Those stormy recollections,
>     Which, be they what they may,
> Are yet the fountain of light of all our day,
> Are yet master light of all our seeing;
>     Uphold us, cherish, and have power to make
> Our noisy years seem moments in the being
> Of the eternal Silence: truths that wake,
>         To perish never;
> Which neither listlessness, nor mad endeavor,
>     Nor all that is at enmity with joy,
> Can utterly abolish or destroy! [33]

Therapy, from this point of view, is an ego-relativizing recollection of the so-called archetypes of the collective unconscious, or more simply a re-engagement of culture.

At this point not Freud, but Norman O. Brown and C. G. Jung become our masters. While Freud's psychoanalytic ambition was abbreviated into the famous dictum: "Where id was, there shall ego be. It is reclamation work, like the draining of the Zuider Zee," [34] Brown affirmed the corollary: Where ego was, there id shall be. Jung, too, took the side of the polymorphously imaginal child of the id, the side of the "unnatural" or "sur-natural" soul, with his theory that beyond the particularity of the personal unconscious lay the archetypes of the collective unconscious, and with his clinical finding that if transference is allowed to elaborate itself freely anything (i.e., a multitude of trans-particular collective contents) can be transferred.

Phone Home!

In the last few decades there has been a proliferation of extra-terrestrial fantasy films — *E. T.*, *Cocoon*, *Starman*, *Taken*, etc. The appeal of these films, I believe, lies in the nostalgia they touch in us for the non-arbitrary form of the subtle body or "sur-natural" soul. The extraterrestrial life forms portrayed in these films, with their strange organs and unique appendages, resonate with the part of us that once wondered, "Why do I have five fingers and not six or three? Why was I born into these particular circumstances?" Is this, then, the background to which we should lead the sense of defectiveness and shame from which our patient's suffer? While usually interpreted as being the result of having been grossly mishandled as children, does this shameful sense of defectiveness also reflect how the preternatural uniqueness of each soul feels on this earth that it has not yet made into world?

Perhaps, one day, Stephen Spielberg will be recognized as a father of psychoanalysis. Let us place his film *E. T.* alongside Anna O. and the Wolfman as a great case in the history of the science (fiction) of soul.

Listening in my chair, I sometimes imagine that the patient in analysis is E. T., the extraterrestrial. His symptoms are his antenna; his complexes, organs that adapt him not to life here but to soul; his transference projections, phone calls to that "imperial palace whence he came." "E. T., phone home" — indeed!

# The Body of Woody

The unnatural, or should I say "sur-natural," soul lives, moves, and has its being, less in the incarnational world of our arbitrary life, than in the imaginal world or constructed world mankind has created for itself in the course of its human process. It is not in our incarnational anatomy of ten fingers and ten toes (and mostly two of everything else) that this soul dwells; the 'body' of the 'sur-natural' soul is the arts of the imagination. In poetry, painting, sculpture, architecture, dance, music, and theater, etc., the sur-natural dimension of the soul finds the range, flexibility and extension necessary for it if it is to reach its full stature. Lear on the heath, the blinded Oedipus, Picasso's minotaur etchings, Duchamp's *Nude Descending a Staircase,* Stravinsky's *Firebird Suite,* a video by the Rolling Stones, Spielberg's *E.T.,* Madonna's song "Like a Virgin" — every character in the world of art and entertainment together make up the fellowship of the sur-natural soul.

The function of theater, in Aristotle's view, is to provide emotional release to the audience, catharsis. A tragedy by Aeschylus, Sophocles, or Euripides arouses in us feelings of pity and fear, develops them to a crescendo point, and absorbs the emotional discharge. From the naturalistic perspective all this is certainly true. Art can be used as vicariously as religion. But from a deeper, unnatural or 'sur-natural' perspective, it is not that our emotional tensions are being vicariously resolved by the wish-world of art; rather, it is the sur-natural soul that is being released from its determinate fetters into the atmosphere of affirmed arbitrariness appropriate to it. The subtle body, the sur-natural soul, breathes fiction. It walks out of the silver screen and re-orders our contingent lives just as Mia Farrow's fictive lover walks out of the movie she is watching in Woody Allen's film, *The Purple Rose of Cairo.* If we wish to understand this occult dimension of the so-called participatory emotions it is to Allen, not to Aristotle, that we will have to turn for guidance.

## Escaping to the Angels

There is an affect that comes *before* creativity and an affect that comes, if it comes at all, only *afterwards*. The first, which cannot be contained or completely experienced due to its traumatic character, splits the psyche and by doing so compels some people to make a creative container in which all that has been split apart can be gathered together again and healed. The second affect, which is sometimes experienced as the apocalyptic unveiling of the first in a burst of repressed affect and insight, corresponds to the actual inhabiting of the container which was formed as a creative defense, and the actual embodiment of the soul which has been made.

Said differently, if taken to the limit, the manic triumph one has achieved over an experience may finally give way to a depressive encounter with it. Although it may take years to find the words to formulate the feelings that could not formerly be borne, it may take still more years before one will allow oneself to be moved by those words. In alchemical terms, the endeavor of finding the so-called "words to say it" corresponds to the *albedo* or "whitening" stage of the process and the being moved by the words, to the *rubedo*, that final stage in which the "soul-work" reddens into life.

But reddening into life is not easy, for the mind, having secured for itself an imaginal or linguistic mastery, reflexively eschews the gasps and sobs through which its words and images could be reconnected to the flesh. Loath to admit the extent to which it feels menaced by that rumble of interior thunder which announces the advent of a feeling-toned complex, the manically whitened mind perseverates more and more grandiloquently. What is sowed in the furrow of denied anxiety, however, cannot be reaped through a similar denial. For it is one thing to "farm ... a verse / [and] make a vineyard of the curse"[35] and quite another to press the grapes and drink the wine.

Avoiding this fact, prolific creativity — be it is transference relationships, work, or art — may become an addiction. Unable to bear what Jung
has called "the terrible ambiguity of direct experience," or, more precisely, in a defensive avoidance of the necessary second encounter with it,
we may live for a time in what could be characterized as an art-for-art's-
sake attitude. Driven by repetition compulsion, the defensively genera-
tive person may only be able to live from project to project, relationship
to relationship, poem to poem in creative inflation. This is diagnostic.
That a person finds it easier to ape God than to be human is the clearest
indication of the rootedness of the manic defense in an archetypal identification. Yet, if the fool would persist in his folly he would become wise.
Being a fatality, such a condition can only be affirmed; healing comes, if
at all, only as a sort of *enatiodromia* brought on by our perilous persistence
in the defensive folly of manic creativity. It will eventually pass.

What goes around comes around. Just as the legendary Parsifal, in
the grail castle for the first time, missed the grail by failing to ask the
fateful question, "Whom does the grail serve?", so many of us miss the
opportunity for our own healing — not once but many times — by failing to ask ourselves what our creative efforts mean to us.

A young man, in the grail castle of his own experience, vividly ex-
emplifies how narrowly the grail can be missed. Although he seems to
ask the decisive question no less that eight times in an eight-line poem,
the aesthetic relief the poem afforded him for the moment *stole the moment*, causing him to miss the eternity or insight, which lay like a treasure
within the moment.

> Can you paint the last stroke in the corner?
> Can you live in your own painted room?
> Can you never the distance to no-where?
> Can you faith say, but never assume?
> Can you sup in the hollows of breathing?
> Can you people the angelic snow?
> Can you dream the world onto a lamb's back?
> Can you love the undammable flow?

In taking so much pleasure in posing them, he never really put his questions to himself, asking what they meant to him personally. This failure to actually grapple with the contents of the unconscious, which have been objectified through the creative process is, of course, indicative of inflation. To the extent that the young man was swept up in the incantational magic of his verse, his awareness of a distinction between the larger Self, which had inspired him, and the little self, to which this inspiration had been addressed, was obliterated.

Jung sometimes characterized a neurosis as a creative phenomenon, an attempt at self-cure that leaves us *all but cured.*[36] Unfortunately, this is only too true. Although creativity plays a vital and necessary role in our healing, and though we may even need to pursue it as an end in itself for a time, it must also be recognized (as deconstruction has shown) that creativity does not deliver us across the fissures of our psychic life to the paradise of any signified. And so, like Prospero at the end of *The Tempest* abjuring his "rough magic," many of us, too, who are psychological *magi,* must eventually abjure ours if we are not to remain trapped in the glitter and illusion of stylized feeling.

It is not just that the trauma from which the psychologically adroit sufferer has fled to the angels of archetypal insight must be faced if that person is to live upon the earth as a human being. The opposite is also the case: the angels through whom one has fled to a traumatized hyper-identity must also be wrestled with. The manic defense itself must be faced if we are to recognize the response of our own essential nature to the impingements we have suffered. For in the deepest sense, our capacity to be traumatized is a secret capacity of the angel who expresses our ambivalence about feeling or refusing to feel a particular event on *a priori* grounds.

"The pearl of great price," a biblical image and archetypal motif many have latched onto to make sense of a long-standing struggle with emotion, is one such angel which refuses, and thereby compensates, the starkness of our lives by sending us on a quest of discovery. Since the motif is rooted in the psyche's inability to represent negation, however, the promise represented by this priceless pearl is actually obtained, if at all, *iconoclastically,* if not quite noniconically, in the deconstruction of the pearl back to the very grit against which it was made — i.e., in the emptiness and despair that we previously could not bear.

T.S. Eliot was right: the end of all our exploring will be to arrive at the place we started and to know it for the first time, *not* merely as a well-wrought poetical construction, but also as the scene of our own crime.

The healing of the split between psyche and soma, the subtle embodiment of each in the other, occurs not in the twinkling of the eye it takes for a manic defense to save us through the repudiation of basic needs but, rather, in that paroxysm of grief in which we actually allow ourselves to be moved by what has been moving us in the form of an archetypal identification or manic defense. And though it may have taken many years to create, with the help of the gods who inspire us, the temple for the soul which Keats describes in his poem, "Ode to Psyche," once it is built, we must also, as Keats tells us in the last line of his poem, learn to leave "a casement open at night, To let the warm Love in." [37]

The End?

The compulsion to repeat, the compulsion to write yet another paragraph on trauma, is not stilled by this arbitrary ending. The problem of trauma can never be finally absorbed. Neither definitive textbooks nor approved gospels can be written. By their very nature traumas are individual and individuating. Like the grit in the oyster that occasions the pearl, overwhelming events tear into the substance of our lives and there start the festering process by which the soul is made.

Traumas are alien particles, just as a fleck of grit, a piece of sand, or a pinch of star-dust are alien particles. When they lodge themselves in our lives as our other, our self-identity is broken and we are alienated from ourselves. Finding ourselves unable to absorb a trauma causes us to become a trauma to ourselves. The simple given-ness of our lives becomes extinct and we must then begin a process of re-creating ourselves. It is in this way that trauma and alienation lead to soul-making.

The work on trauma is a repetition compulsion of ceaseless mental fight. Interminable analysis, interminable writing, interminable soul-making is the only medicine — there is no antidote. The transmuting of trauma into creative affirmations, the mutual transformation of trauma and soul, is a process that like poetry "survives in the valley of its own saying."[38] To put it another way . . . and another way . . . and another way is what soul-making is all about.

1. As cited by Erich Neumann in *The Origins and History of Consciousness* (Princeton, N.J.: Princeton University Press, 1973), p. 401.

2. Cited by Ernest Becker, *The Denial of Death* (New York: Free Press, 1973), p. 262.

3. Sigmund Freud, *Three Essays on the Theory of Sexuality*, in SE 7: 226n.

4. C.G. Jung, CW 4: 780.

5. Donald W. Winnicott, "The Psychology of Madness," in *Psychoanalytic Explorations*, C. Winnicott, R. Shepherd, M. Davis, eds. (Cambridge, MA.: Harvard University Press, 1992), p. 122.

6. Donald W. Winnicott, "Fear of Breakdown," in ibid., pp. 87–95.

7. C.G. Jung, CW 9.1: 304.

8. Ibid.

9. Cf. James Hillman, *The Soul's Code: In Search of Character and Calling* (New York: Warner Books, 1996).

10. C.G. Jung, CW 17: 97.

11. William Wordsworth, "Ode: Intimations of Immortality," lines 80-85.

12. Ibid., lines 49-57..

13. Sigmund Freud and Joseph Breuer, "On the Theory of Hysterical Attacks," CP, 5: 30.

14. C. G. Jung, CW 16: 449.

15. Samuel Taylor Coleridge, *Biographia Literaria*, vol. 1: 80–81.

16. My references to "negativizing" or "interiorizing" things "into themselves" (rather than into ourselves) draws upon Wolfgang Giegerich's introduction of logical negativity into psychology. See his *The Soul's Logical Life* (Frankfurt am Main: Peter Lang, 1998).

17. C.G. Jung, CW 8: 423.

18. C.G. Jung, CW 4: 764.

19. C.G. Jung, CW 4: 665.

20. C.G. Jung, CW 17: 97.

21. In this connection we may be reminded of Donald Kalsched's account of what he calls the archetypal self-care system. Under the duress of early trauma the personality, in Kalsched's view, may split itself apart in such a way as to create a persecutory figure. This figure, in turn, "protects" what he calls the "personal spirit" from the dreaded possibility that life will bring still further hurt and trauma by carrying out inhibition-producing internal attacks of its own upon the subject. See his *The Inner World of Trauma: Archetypal Defenses of the Personal Spirit* (London: Routledge, 1996).

22. C.G. Jung CW 14: 778.

23. Coleridge, *Biographia Literaria*, vol. 2: 273.

24. C.G. Jung, CW 10: 655.

25. C.G. Jung, CW 9.1: 217.

26. C.G. Jung, CW 16: 534.

27. C.G. Jung, CW 4: 737.

28. James Hillman, *The Soul's Code*, pp. 41–62.

29. C.G. Jung, *Memories, Dreams, Reflections*, p. 9, italics mine.

30. Ibid., p. 10.

31. Ibid, pp. 16–17.

32. Ibid, p. 90.

33. William Wordsworth, "Ode: Intimations of Immortality from Recollections of Early Childhood," lines 138–61.

34. Sigmund Freud, *New Introductory Lectures on Psycho-Analysis*, in *SE* 22: 80.

35. W.H. Auden, "In Memory of W.B. Yeats." In *Collected Poems*, ed. Edward Mendelson (London/New York: Faber/Random House, 1976), p. 198.

36. C.G. Jung, CW 10: 361.

37. John Keats, "Ode to Psyche," in *Selected Poems and Letters*, p. 205.

38. W.H. Auden, "In Memory of W.B. Yeats," op. cit., p. 197.

GREG MOGENSON is a Jungian analyst practicing in London, Ontario, Canada. The author of many articles in the field of analytical psychology, his books include *The Dove in the Consulting Room: Hysteria and the Anima in Bollas and Jung; Northern Gnosis: Thor, Baldr, and the Volsungs in the Thought of Freud and Jung; Greeting the Angels: An Imaginal View of the Mourning Process;* and (with Wolfgang Giegerich and David L. Miller) *Dialectics & Analytical Psychology: The El Capitan Canyon Seminar.* The present volume, *A Most Accursed Religion,* is an extensively revised and expanded version of his first book, *God Is a Trauma: Vicarious Religion and Soul-Making.*